"I am fully in agreement ⟨...⟩ need to 'reboot' much of ⟨...⟩ The main focus of the b⟨...⟩ technology in school to i⟨...⟩ eloquently says - the curre⟨...⟩ long-term damage in ever⟨...⟩ help you make some key c⟨...⟩ ⟨...⟩ you prioritise your spending in a cash-strapped system"

**Dave Harris, Author of *Brave Heads*,
retired headteacher and education consultant**

"Despite the enthusiasm and activity of passionate individuals and associations for more than 35 years, we are still trying to shoehorn modern education technologies into a 19th century system and it doesn't work! In this book, '*Reboot*', Jay and Charlotte offer practical solutions on well argued theoretical underpinnings that have the potential to transform schools, not overnight but steadily and sustainably. So, in a system that is showing clear signs of increased stresses and is also in danger of becoming irrelevant to the needs and experiences of learners it's time to take action, put people at the centre and reboot!"

Mark Chambers, CEO Naace

"The impact has been just huge, it has been enormous, and the impact of that has been we are able to implement strategies very quickly into our school. It's opened up a world where we can take our knowledge and skills and embed them thoroughly across the school."

**Caroline Beaumont, Headteacher, Parkroyal
Community Primary School**

Reboot

How we must rethink the use of technology in education to truly revolutionise our schools

JAY ASHCROFT
with CHARLOTTE GREEN

Reboot:
How we must rethink the use of technology in education to truly revolutionise our schools
By Jay Ashcroft with Charlotte Green

Education | Leadership

First published 2017

Cover illustration by Bikelindo V. Rouco

The rights of Jay Ashcroft and Charlotte Green to be identified as the authors of this work have been asserted in accordance with Sections 77 and 78 of the Copyright Designs and Patents Act, 1988.

All rights reserved. No part of this book may be reproduced in material (including photocopying or storing in any medium by electronic means and whether or not transiently or incidentally to some other use of this publication) without the written permission of the copyright holder except in accordance with the provisions of the Copyright, Designs and Patents Act 1988. Applications for Copyright holders written permission to reproduce any part of this publication should be addressed to hello@learnmaker.co.uk

This book is available to order online from amazon.co.uk

Copyright 2017 Jay Ashcroft with Charlotte Green

Please Note: This book is intended for information only and does not constitute legal, financial or specific professional advice unique to your situation. The Author, Publisher and Resellers accept no responsibility for loss, damage or injury to persons or their belongings as a direct or indirect result of reading this book.

DEDICATION

This book is dedicated to the people who go out into the world to make a difference. Through your hardwork and commitment we all live on a better planet.

CONTENTS

Introduction — 1

PART 1: WHY RETHINK THE USE OF TECHNOLOGY?

1. The Challenges of Improving Education — 9
2. The LearnMaker Method — 25

PART 2: NEW WAYS TO USE TECHNOLOGY

3. Principle One: Improving Capability of Teachers (Part 1) — 35
4. Principle One: Improving the Capability of your Team (Part 2) — 51
5. Principle Two: Improving the Productivity of Schools — 63
6. Principle Three: Improving the Consistency of Lessons — 103

PART 3: REBOOTING YOUR SCHOOL

7. Environment Dictates Technology	125
8. The Time to Act is Now	143
One Final Thing	159
Bibliography	161
Acknowledgements	163
About the Author	165
The Accelerated School Improvement Programme	167
Additional Resources	170
A Final Ask	172

Introduction

One billion pounds has been spent on technology in schools in the UK in the last five years, and yet all research indicates that it has had no tangible impact on student progress. Classrooms today are filled with interactive whiteboards, tablets and laptops, yet standards of education are no better than they were prior to these devices. When the government announces more spending cuts in education, school leaders react understandably with outrage and dismay, and insist that they are already struggling to meet the demands of the education system with their current budget. However, at a cost of $149,743 (PISA studies use US dollars as the currency of choice) per child through their school journey, only four countries in the world spend more than the UK on education (Luxembourg, Switzerland, Norway, and Denmark, as of early 2017).

In all other areas of life, technology exists to make our lives easier. It saves time and performs tasks more efficiently. Yet, the average teacher in a UK school now works fifty-nine hours per week, and many complain that technology has complicated their professional life. This begs the question: if schools are so cash-strapped why are they spending so much money on something that has so little impact? I have been working in the UK education system for seven years now, and one thing is clear: things aren't adding up.

If you want to understand a school's relationship with technology, there is a quick and easy way to achieve this: look in its cupboards. During my visits to schools up and down the UK, I've seen enough wasted technology gathering dust on shelves to bring me out in a cold sweat. I know of a secondary school that has £100,000 worth of iPads sitting idle, a primary school with three unused professional-grade cameras at a cost of £46,000, and another primary that owns £20,000 of unused Star Wars BB8 robots, one for every child in the class. All of this technology was bought on the premise that it would help children learn. Learn from it they certainly can: don't spend £20,000 of your school budget on robots, kids!

These neglected gadgets are a dire symptom of a much deeper problem: schools have become unproductive and inefficient, and as a result, struggle to maximise students' and teachers' potential. The result of this is that teachers feel overwhelmed, overworked and under-appreciated. Worse still, students are not getting the education they deserve.

I founded my company, *LearnMaker*, because I wanted to effect real change within the education system and recognised that my job as an education technology salesperson was only making it more complicated. That's why, in 2014, I quit my career and started a consultancy firm to help schools to accelerate their improvement by getting to the bottom of their technological and organisational problems.

My philosophy for using technology to accelerate school improvement is simple. Any piece of technology that is implemented should be dedicated to improving the performance of teachers. This flies in the face of how educational technology has been used for three decades now because, bar a few exceptions, almost all of it has been targeted towards the classroom learning experience. By this, I mean apps for students to use in the classroom, touchscreen displays and trolleys upon trolleys of laptops. This strategy can work, and mobile devices such as the iPad offer schools a huge opportunity to deliver learning in new and innovative ways, but they will only do so if they have been implemented properly and teachers are skilled at using them. In other words, technology is not a silver bullet when it comes to student progress. Technology can accelerate performance gains, but it is not enough to start them.

Transforming education using iPads, for example, requires you to use them to rebuild the systems and processes within your school. This includes redeveloping the curriculum, the assessment system and even the way teachers deliver lessons. Redeveloping any one of these is a huge undertaking, so to do all three is beyond all but the most dedicated and resourceful schools. That's why only a handful in the UK can claim to have transformed student outcomes with the help of technology such as the iPad. I know many of these schools and I can safely say they're outliers. They don't represent the norm. With this in mind, it is time to reassess how we view technology in school and begin targeting it towards those who do make the difference in the classroom: teachers.

You may feel there is no pressing need to put my advice into practice in your school. I meet many who are ticking along just fine and some that are excelling, but if you think that the issue of improving teaching and learning is only for the 'average' institution, you'd be wrong. I have seen first hand how even the most successful and highly-rated schools can be transformed by improving how they use technology. In 2015, I worked with an Outstanding rated school who are accredited by The National College of Teaching and Leadership. The school is, by any measure, an example for others to follow, and the teaching and learning experiences for children there are exceptional. Students' work is put on display in a national museum and they've been featured on big screens across the city. However, after working with them for twelve weeks, my strategies significantly improved the level at which their teachers could perform. I supported them to remove inefficient systems and implement better ones, making it simpler for teachers to perform their job, and to a higher standard. The outcome? Senior leaders at the school freed up four extra hours in their working week, teachers freed up an extra ninety minutes per week and the school has already saved £30,000 within twelve months.

In this book, I will explore the concepts and methodologies of how you can transform the performance of your own school by focusing on how technology can aid your teachers.

Jay

PART 1

[WHY RETHINK THE USE OF TECHNOLOGY?]

CHAPTER 1

The Challenges of Improving Education

"We must take change by the hand or rest assuredly, change will take us by the throat."
Winston Churchill

I refreshed the inbox just to make sure. My eyes weren't deceiving me. LearnMaker had been shortlisted for the 2016 Naace Impact Award, the most prestigious award in the edtech (educational technology) industry. Our project had transformed an underperforming secondary school maths department in ten weeks using iPads. We trained the teachers to use iPads for assessment, and by the end of our time with them, had reduced their marking cycle from two weeks to two days, increased student and teacher interactions by 300%, and improved independent working by 87%. At the end of the year, student GCSE progress was up by 25%. I had received coverage for the work from as far away as Dubai, received numerous invitations to present on the education speaking circuit and, suffice to say, the buzz created by the project would have been enough to keep offers of work coming in for the next few years. Yet, something didn't feel right, and for me the achievement felt hollow. I'd heard through the grapevine that the foundations laid for teachers in the maths department were slowly being dismantled in favour of returning to the old way of doing things. They were happy to have seen the improvements. However, once the project was finished, the school went back to its usual ways because it felt familiar. Worse still, they took the iPads out of the hands of teachers and made them a bookable resource for students to use, with the idea that this was 'better'.

Unfortunately, this wasn't the first time I had seen this happen. I had been working to improve learning with technology in the UK education system for eighteen months by then and, in that time, had worked with Apple and Google, and received accreditation by the Department of Education. Month after month,

I would meet new schools that wanted to know how to use technology to enhance learning. Each time, I would offer my insight and guidance, only to find that few actually took it. Rather than looking to transform how teachers worked, school leaders wanted lesson ideas, apps to use and projects to run, all focused on the classroom. Despite my best efforts, they couldn't accept that focusing on technology in this way was a false economy.

Schools wanted the wow factor that technology brought to the classroom, and were prepared to ignore just how little it affected student learning.

What is it, then, that schools really need to enhance teaching and learning? My experience in the education system, has led me to an exciting and inescapable conclusion that prompted me to write this book. For a school to flourish, it must focus on developing the performance of its teachers day after day. Technology can accelerate the performance of teachers in new and inspiring ways and this is why it must be focused towards them first. Only then will teaching and learning improve.

This book explores this concept in depth, and discusses the three key principles that you will need to employ if you want to develop technology as a means for improving student progress. To do this you must focus on improving three key areas: the capability of teachers, the productivity of the school, and consistency of lessons.

Improving the capability of teachers enables them to deliver outstanding lessons and have more one-to-one interaction with students; improving productivity reduces the time and energy spent on paperwork and administration so that staff can get on with what really matters; finally, improving consistency of lessons means that quality can be driven higher and higher. These are not breakthrough new concepts, and they're already a focus in a number of schools I meet. The problem is that they're being developed through multiple initiatives and plans, and this is where the wheels fall off. To bring about a radical transformation, you must commit to one goal, in this case, improving teaching and learning, and deliver it through one means. Only then will everyone in your school get behind it and give it traction.

If you want your school to excel, you should make it your goal to improve how well teachers can perform, and I believe the means to deliver that is through technology. Don't mistake the order: the goal must always come before the means. Technology is never a goal, and this is where schools get lost. Schools often say they buy technology with the goal to improve student outcomes, but when pushed most are unable to give any specific ways in which it will do so beyond 'improving engagement'. That's a clear sign that buying technology was the goal in the first place, because it's not linked to any educational benefit. Don't fall into that trap.

The tipping point

SCHOOL IMPROVEMENT IS a huge topic, and so wide and varied that it can become a little overwhelming. There are numerous organisations, conferences and platforms all dedicated to the question of how best to improve schools. Each one will give you different, and sometimes contradictory, advice, and you reach a point where you have so many ideas and so much information that the most difficult part becomes picking a route to embark upon.

The tipping point is a simple idea. In every organisation, there is one central element that has a huge amount of untapped potential. Connected with everything in your school, if you can unlock its potential you will transform the entire performance because it starts a domino chain. By explicitly improving just one central element, you implicitly improve everything around it.

For a school, the tipping point is the quality of the teaching. This is central to all success, and interlinked with everything that happens throughout. If you explicitly improve the performance of teachers, then this will implicitly improve student assessment, safeguarding and countless other strategies that schools focus on. Instead of dividing your resources and energy between numerous goals, collectively place it all behind one goal, and you will greatly increase your chances of achieving it.

It's rather like five people trying to push eight boulders up a hill. It's hard to conjure an image of how exactly these poor souls would achieve this, and the likely outcome is that they will fail. Now, picture the same five people, collectively pushing just one larger boulder up the same hill: a much easier challenge for them to succeed at. It's an obvious analogy, but for anyone who has worked in education consultancy, a poignant one also. Schools are overrun with well-meant initiatives that require more man hours than exist in a working day. There is no better example of this than the six-pen marking system that has swept across primary schools like wildfire since 2011. With each colour denoting a different competency or ability, teachers spend hours per week working to this system despite it never having been a requirement. Moreover, there is no evidence to suggest it benefits the student. Similarly, secondary schools adopted the 'triple marking' system, which allows students to respond to teacher comments. In principle it's a sound idea, but in reality it often means students don't receive returned work and a final mark for until up to two weeks later. Such a delay offsets the benefits that it provides. Teachers are left undertaking extra work for no extra benefit.

Schools select a number of the most important goals and assign them to members of their leadership team. However, you quickly find that there are more goals than there are people to assign them to and that's where improvement initiatives fall down. You may be blessed with a large enough team to delegate to, but then the challenge becomes ensuring everyone is on the same page and working to the same end outcome. This presents its own problems.

This is why it is better to identify your tipping point and unify behind that single goal.

The trouble following targets

WHEN SCHOOLS TAKE their lead from external influences like Ofsted and results tables, they have a tendency to focus on output alone, in the form of exam results, Ofsted rating and attendance records. This sounds like a reasonable strategy, because these elements are what schools' reputations rest on, in the eyes of these bodies.

However, the problem comes when schools focus on these alone. The reality is you can't improve a school's output in the long-term without improving the system in which it is created. This becomes even more problematic when you consider the current environment in education in the UK. The onus is on teachers to do most of the grafting in schools, without appropriate support from systems and processes to lighten their workload. Moreover, schools are reluctant to invest in anything that doesn't have an instant impact, precisely because of the pressures put on them by external bodies to satisfy certain criteria. Add these factors together, and what you are left with is a culture of inefficiency that is slow to move forwards.

The challenges that schools face have slowly crept up on them. As demands grow on an organisation, operations and strategic thinking must come into play to ensure that employees are not swamped and can react to changes, but in education this simply hasn't happened. It has left schools ill-equipped and unprepared for the challenges of today.

Short-term interventions equal long-term problems

THERE IS NO shortcut to improving learning in your school. You can achieve a short-term spike in results with quick-fix measures (often at the expense of long term success), or you can achieve long-term success with an in-depth, holistic approach. Nothing demonstrates the perils of the quick fix more clearly than the modern phenomenon of the so-called 'superhead'. The term superhead is used to describe a headteacher who is appointed to a failing school in order to improve standards. They are typically seen as having outstanding qualities as a leader, are come well-regarded with a reputation that precedes them. Their ability to transform schools on the brink of closure into Outstanding-rated beacons of success is certainly impressive, and has probably helped to save schools that might otherwise have closed permanently. The news headlines and Department of Education accolades do not tell the whole story, however.

Researchers at the Centre for High Performance observed 160 academies over five years, including twenty-one schools with a superhead. At first glance, the study appears to suggest that they are the secret to success: the academies with superheads in charge oversaw greater immediate improvements than the rest. However, what this research also brings to light is the questionable methods employed by the superheads employed during their tenures. All but one of the twenty-one superheads in the study moved their outstanding teachers into year 11, the GCSE year group, boosting the chances of that age group performing well, but also depriving younger children access to outstanding teaching until their final year. All of the superheads focused specifically on maths and English, often at the expense of arts subjects and extracurricular activities, and excluded poorly behaving students. Eighteen out of twenty-one didn't enter low-ability pupils into exams unless parents agreed to educate them at home.

I find this troubling because I don't believe that academically able children have a higher 'value' than those who find themselves on grade boundaries. Likewise, I don't believe that certain subjects should be given precedence over others.

The real cost of the short-term gains achieved by these methods becomes clear when you see what happened to these academies once the superheads departed. Results fell on average by 6%. The longer they stayed in a school, the worse the impact was when they left. Those staying for three years or longer saw results fall by an average of 9% when they departed. Not surprising when you consider that the schools' resources were channelled towards the students that 'mattered' the most in terms of immediate targets, the GCSE year group. It cost the twenty-one academies in the study a staggering £11.8 million in consultancy fees to rectify the damage left behind by these tactics.

By contrast, the academies without superheads outperformed their counterparts at the five-year mark. Improvement was slower, but there were no exam result crashes or any need to bring in external consultants.

Superheads command salaries starting at £70,000 in primary schools and £100,000 in secondaries. The high premium that schools pay for this kind of leadership could be better spent, in my opinion. Focusing on targets helped these schools in the short term, but left them with a host of problems to unpick once those targets had been met.

The evidence is clear: you can't achieve long-term success with a short-term mindset.

Investing in the long term

A CHARITY SETS a goal to provide fresh, clean water to communities in Africa. How should it achieve this end?

One way would be to send out thousands of bottles of water. The other would be to build wells in these communities and teach locals the skills to build more. We don't even have to think about the options: we know that building wells is the right choice. This is because we understand the power of infrastructure and the right skills when it comes to something as life and death as water. The short-term option seems ludicrous by comparison.

Now contrast education. The goal is to help students achieve higher grades. The short-term option would be to buy new learning resources, classroom technology or hire support staff. The long-term option would be to invest in the school's systems and infrastructure so that staff can complete their jobs to a higher standard and become more efficient. Like the bottled water example, the option of learning resources, technology and support staff requires a constant stream of money to ensure it continues to achieve the outcome. The second option requires greater investment in the short-term, but once established, will create a culture of excellence and cost less to maintain.

Strangely, it is easier for most people to see the disparity between the two options in the charity analogy than in this second example. No charity in its right mind would send bottled water en masse rather than build a well! So, why is it harder to picture what long-term investment looks like for a school, and to justify choosing this over better-known methods?

The sad truth is that there is no clear picture for those within education of what it means to invest long term. All the most popular initiatives intended to boost attainment are focused on the here and now. Even if a school had the urge to buck this trend, how would it go about it?

One of the underlying principles of this book is that in order to improve your school, you will need to focus on investing in the future and ignore the temptation of the quick fix. If you have the foresight to dedicate time and money into nurturing a culture of efficiency and high standards, then this will reap far more than any number of gadgets or new learning resources ever could. The needs of your students and pressures on educators are constantly shifting, and the demands you'll face next year will be different from those of today. If you're not committing money to develop your organisation, you will be left unprepared for the changes that are coming.

Expecting the unexpected

SCHOOLS ARE ORGANIC organisations and this is true whether you're a village primary or an inner city secondary: every day brings something new and unpredictable to the table. It can be as simple as a student forgetting their bag through to a teacher calling in sick; a fight in the playground through to a lack of teabags in the staff room. No two days are the same in a school and this is what makes working in education so enjoyable.

However, the flip side of this is that the job can also be very draining. While variety is certainly interesting, the sheer amount of unexpectedness and unpredictability that can happen on any given day in a school can leave teachers mentally fatigued and burnt out. Education policy has placed intense pressure on many staff to ensure student targets are met in the modern school, while a culture of paperwork and student data leaves teachers time poor. This is where the school organisation must pick up the slack to protect those who work inside it. If you improve capability, productivity and consistency across your school, the stress of a teacher's job is better spread meaning they can become far more effective. It is the leadership's job to create an environment that protects those in the classroom and brings meaning to the work everyone is doing. Adversity is no problem when you are filled with belief in your purpose. Better tools and support to develop your teachers' capability will improve their classroom performance. Better productivity will save staff time and energy, allowing them to complete their work quicker and with less effort. Higher consistency in lessons will drive up the quality of teaching and learning, and result in better student outcomes over time.

When these three principles are in place, all staff across a school can satisfy the demands of their job with less stress, energy and time, and when that happens you can focus on developing the quality of their teaching. Higher quality equals better outcomes, and this is how you really drive a school's performance over time.

It's time to get going

THERE IS NO shortage of passion and commitment in the education system. In some people these qualities may be hidden, beaten down from years of stress and long hours, but they are always there, hiding, waiting to be unearthed again. As a school leader, you need to create the environment in your school where these hidden qualities can flourish. The best part is that you get to choose when you start your school's development. It may take some work if you're stuck in the trenches at war with paperwork and administration, but it can be done. It's one of the reasons why you became a headteacher: to make a difference and lead your school. I'm yet to meet a school leader who took on the role because they just loved filling out forms and looking at spreadsheets!

Think of every technology fad, intervention and 'pioneering' strategy to improve standards you have come across in your time in education (think computer suites, interactive whiteboards, and iPads) and ask yourself how effective they have been. As the list grows in your mind, take note of any memories that spring to the fore of how you or others felt about these interventions. Were you hopeful, full of expectation, or feeling vaguely cautious? Try writing them down, and include side notes about the measurable impact they had.

Committing this to paper will allow you to visualise just how many technologies gain traction in education in the name of improving student outcomes, and how little they have achieved. If you choose to action the three principles in this book, it will be important to keep this list and its meagre impact in mind, because you will be doing so in a market in which schools are constantly being tempted to invest in the latest 'big idea' in technology. There are no points for actioning fifty percent of the method that I will share in the following chapters and you won't improve student progress until all three principles are in place.

It is important to note that on your journey towards improvement you will come up against many distractions. You'll go to educational conferences, speak with fellow heads and see articles in the publications you read, all shouting about the new big breakthrough in learning. It might be a new classroom technique, a new assessment strategy or a new piece of technology on the market. Schools will flock to embrace it and this will leave you with your first big challenge: staying on the path. The temptation to follow the latest trend may be strong, but you need to ask yourself if it is really for you. The people championing the trend are often the ones who've pioneered it, who've spent years preparing and working with it until it fits their need. You don't see how they got to where they are, only the success it comes with, and that is not the whole story.

This may be unnerving but it is the reality of success. The schools that lead the way are those that solve their own needs. They spend years crafting and developing themselves unnoticed, and then one day they are thrust into the spotlight as an exemplar for all others to follow. With commitment and determination, that can be your school. In the next chapters you will find out how to get there.

CHAPTER 2

The LearnMaker Method

"If you are not willing to risk the usual, you will have to settle for the ordinary."

Jim Rohn

Every school we have worked with at LearnMaker has enabled me to gain a deeper insight into what is missing in the quest for school improvement. I've been lucky enough to work with educators from around the globe, and regardless of geography or demographics, I keep hearing about the same challenges back from school leaders. They consistently state that lack of time, lack of money and changing policy are all barriers holding back their school's improvement.

These three external challenges occur repeatedly across multiple education systems, including countries that consistently outperform their peers. This is significant, because it shows that money, time or policy change are not the performance inhibitors in education. If they were, then no school would excel. The reality is that UK schools are some of the most richly funded in the entire world. More is spent on education in the UK than all but four countries globally, and yet as of 2015, the UK ranks 15th in the International PISA findings. The problems that schools in this country face, then, can't be attributed solely to government intervention.

These insights, and my years of experience working with schools, have led me to a worrying conclusion: external challenges in the education system are disproportionately impacting on how well teachers perform in the classroom, in part because school organisations are too technologically underdeveloped to protect themselves. The introduction of Progress 8 and Attainment 8 are the latest developments that will really test a school's systems and processes. Already I'm meeting teachers who are being tasked by school leadership with evidencing everything students do, yet this isn't what Progress 8 is about. Ofsted will be looking for how decisions are made on how to drive student progress from the data that is captured. There are plenty of new assessment platforms available that easily allow a school to do this, yet it requires a move away from the traditional stalwarts, that for some, have become as much a part of the school as the building itself. The difficulty is that while the traditional platforms are well developed in capturing data and evidence, they have little to no functionality when it comes to automating analysis and spotting trends. This is what Ofsted will be looking at, and what schools will increasing be judged on in the coming years. There will be no prizes for the most data or evidence captured.

To counteract these challenges and enable teachers to do their best work, I developed the LearnMaker Method that consists of the development of three key principles across a school. We improve the capability of teachers by giving them new ways of working and better tools, we improve the productivity of the school by reducing the time and energy spent on paperwork and administration, and we improve the consistency of lessons, so that a baseline of performance is established which can be improved upon year after year.

This method comes together in the form of a improvement programme that schools can work with us on. We only work with a handful of schools at any one time because it is an intensive process and every school's journey is unique. While we always focus on the same three elements, our programmes are bespoke to the schools we work with. What works for one may not be helpful for another, and there is no 'blueprint for improvement' that can be copied and pasted from one school onto another. I believe the best educational experiences will always be shaped by teachers. Improving the effectiveness of teachers and the whole school, through the use of technology, is the ethos that LearnMaker's school improvement programmes are built upon.

How this book will help you

THIS BOOK WILL guide you through the three principles of the LearnMaker Method, so that by the time you have finished reading, you will understand what is required of you and your leadership team in order to improve your school through the use of technology. I will explain chapter by chapter why focussing on capability, productivity, and consistency is vital and how you should begin to make plans to improve all three areas in your school.

What makes this book different from others in the field is that it benefits not only from my years of contact with schools, but also from my experience working at Apple, one of the most successful and innovative companies on the planet. When I was 23, I began working in their corporate division as a team manager in one of their flagship stores. I was new to the industry, having left behind a career as a music teacher. I remember feeling out of my depth on my first day, and wondering whether I would be able to perform to the level of my peers, who had been managing sales teams for years. It was a highly competitive and demanding environment, in a company that had no time for slow learners. As it turned out, I loved the challenges it presented me with, and I was pretty good at it too. It taught me, beyond all other things, that when you put a lot of effort into a task, you must have something to show for it. Working long hours is not the same thing as doing a good job, in the same way that managing a team of staff to sell 100 iPads per day is not good enough, if they are capable of selling 200.

From the first day, I was fascinated to understand how to develop my team's capabilities, their productivity and the consistency of their sales' performance. I observed what was happening on the sales floor, and by focussing on these three elements, I developed one of the best performing teams in Europe. I now want to bring that knowledge back into education and help schools excel. I meet teachers who put in Herculean efforts on a daily basis for their students, but who don't always get the results they should, for all that commitment and passion. I want to change that.

This is not about trying to superimpose a business model over a school. I couldn't think of anything worse! What I offer is the knowledge and guidance to help you put three simple principles in place that will transform how well teachers can perform. All without compromising any of the values that make education so unique.

By the end of this book, you will understand what you need to do in order to improve your own school significantly and create an exceptional learning environment. This book will talk you through the three principles that I consider to this: capability of staff, productivity of school and consistency of lessons.

It is important to note that these principles must be focused on in this order, because each principle is the foundation of the next in the series. For example, you cannot raise the productivity of your school if you haven't given teachers the tools they need to be more capable. Neither can you effectively raise the consistency of lessons if staff are time poor, as the school will be inefficient and unable to achieve this.

I wrote this book because I believe that in the conversation about school improvement, these three principles have been sorely neglected. It is not about creating a method to satisfy Ofsted, or learning how to 'work the system'; it is about creating an environment that makes it easier for people to excel in their jobs, protects your staff and offers solutions when difficulties arise. It will prepare you for the future, even if you have no idea what that might look like.

Activity: The LearnMaker Scorecard

WHAT CAN BE measured can be improved, which is why I've created a free assessment tool that will score your own school across the three principles covered in this book.

It's all too easy to read on and think 'that's nice but it doesn't really apply to my school' so before going any further take five minutes out and complete the LearnMaker scorecard by going to www.learnmaker.co.uk/scorecard

Once complete, you will receive a customised report that will give you have a better picture of where you are right now and what to focus on to improve further.

PART 2
NEW WAYS TO USE TECHNOLOGY

CHAPTER 3

Principle One: Improving Capability of Teachers (Part 1)

"Technology is nothing. What's important is that you have a faith in people, that they're basically good and smart, and if you give them tools, they'll do wonderful things with them."
Steve Jobs

Martin was a man on the brink. Bleary-eyed and with a knot in his gut, he clenched and unclenched a fist, the thought of the school bell making his shoulders twitch. He looked ahead of him at the queue for the photocopier. The line of teachers was ten long, and he was languishing at the back, caught in the no man's land between the fire exit and the staffroom stash of Jammie Dodgers. He grimaced, understanding that his decision to have an extra cup of coffee this morning had cost him dear. It was 8.47 and, judging by Mrs Harrison's snail's pace at the photocopier, those worksheets he had laboured over the night before would never see the light of day.

I like to call this vignette 'Photocopier of Doom'. I think it tells something of the tragedy and farce of the daily battles that some teachers have become embroiled in, all in an effort to carry out the basic tasks of their job. I have seen teachers deprive themselves of sleep to be at the head of the photocopying queue, and others broker alliances with support staff and fellow teachers to share the burden of copying sheets. Others still play a form of brinkmanship, arriving at the photocopier with only minutes to spare before the 9am bell. This strategic dance is endemic in schools across the UK. Perhaps you are reading this as you wait in line, with one eye on the print button!

So, how do photocopying woes relate to the teaching capability of your team? From everything I have witnessed in schools, it has become clear to me that issues like photocopying queues are symptomatic of a much greater malaise. The most basic tasks in schools are eating into teachers' schedules and creating inefficiencies that impact on how well they can do their job. Teachers do not have the time and space they need to create high quality teaching resources, or to have the one-on-one contact with students that would aid their learning. Teachers who are capable of transforming a student's learning experience are being distracted and waylaid by inefficient and ineffective processes.

This was certainly the case at Parkroyal Primary School, a school based in the north of England where the simple act of photocopying resources had become a drain on staff morale. The senior leadership team had identified that they had reached a plateau when there were no more hours in the day to work. They had a very clear vision of what learning could look like in their classrooms, yet they had no other framework to reach it other than through hard work. When working hard didn't get them there they began questioning how they could work smarter. This led the school to work with LearnMaker, and they committed to moving to the cloud by adopting Google Suite for Education as a foundation on which to develop their school. Visit Parkroyal today and you'll find that not only have achieved their original vision, they've gone far beyond it and are now at a place that they didn't think was possible. They didn't get there by working harder or even spending more money. They simply choose a better vehicle to take them there: they choose cloud technology.

To improve the standard of teaching in your school, you must enable your team to collaborate on teaching resources and to create a system that allows staff to personalise learning for students. Moreover, you must endeavour to rid your school of outdated and inefficient systems that take valuable time from teachers. In this chapter, I will share with you how all of these goals, and many more, are achievable through the effective use of technology.

Capability is a broad topic so I have covered it in two parts. The first focuses on increasing the capability of individual teachers; the second looks at ways to improve the capability of your overall team.

Living on Cloud 9

THE IMPROVEMENTS THAT many schools seek simply aren't attainable through working harder or even an increased budget. It is key that you begin using the time and money available to you more efficiently. Technology is the tool to enable you to do this because when used correctly it enables you to get more out than you put in.

For most schools, in the current environment a teacher puts one hour into lesson planning and they get one hour of resources out. This means that 1 hour in equals 1 hour out.

The situation is no different when it comes to money. Schools primarily use money to hire more staff.

If we imagine one teacher produces 50 hours of work per week, to get 100 hours out we would need two teachers. To get 5000 out we would need 10 teachers and so on. So what happens when you need more hours out than you have time or money to put in I hear you ask? The system breaks, and this is exactly where we are at in education right now.

When I first met Parkroyal Community Primary School, based in Crewe, teachers were maxing out their working hours and the school budget was running at its limit. They had nothing more to put in, so they couldn't get anything more out. Working with LearnMaker, we implemented a platform called Google Suite for Education (G Suite) to change this. G Suite is one of the leading cloud technologies and works by storing documents online in the 'cloud'. It has a long list of features such as office software, document sharing and instant messaging apps that enable teachers to collaborate and communicate effortlessly, and being able to work together online, without needing to be in the same room at the same time, is a significant force multiplier for any school.

Adopting the latest technology in your school might have you fretting about the bank balance, so how would you react if I told you that G Suite is completely free? It is a transformational piece of technology, available to any school without cost, and should have any school leader chomping at the bit. To my surprise, I have found that there is a reluctance within school leadership teams to adopt G Suite, perhaps because it is unfamiliar and represents a complete shift towards a new way of working. It could be that headteachers doubt that cloud software could resolve the myriad of issues they face (heavy workload, reams of homework to mark and long working hours to name but a few). I want to use Parkroyal's example to show you that these doubts are unfounded.

Working Collaboratively

FIFTEEN WEEKS AFTER we'd implemented G Suite with Parkroyal, the printing queue at 8am was a thing of the past. My strategy was to improve collaboration so that staff could work and plan together. We took all lesson planning online and created a shared bank of leadership-approved resources for teachers to use. Even though staff had thousands of worksheets and activities available to them, printing drastically decreased. This was because teachers began working together online, developing long-term learning journeys for their students and planning lessons weeks in advance. Prior to installing cloud software, there was simply little to no time in the school day to sit down with peers or to develop lessons plans and curriculum resources. Instead, teachers were working in isolation, creating or downloading what resources they could late at night before printing them off the following day. A 'worksheet' culture had crept in because teachers simply didn't have the capacity to develop work more than a week or so in advance. G Suite enabled them to begin working collaboratively at home.

If you are doubtful about the benefits of close collaboration, then it is useful to look at the example of Finland, consistently ranked as one of the best education system in the world in the eyes of the OECD (Organisation for Economic Cooperation and Development). I'm fascinated by the Finnish education system and how it developed its exceptional standards. The answer to their success is complex, but I believe two factors are key. The first is cultural and is something no other country can replicate. Teaching is one of the most valued professions in Finland, a far cry from how most teachers in the UK feel about their role. However, the second factor is environmental and something from which we can learn a lot. Finnish teachers only spend 600 hours in the classroom per year, an average of four lessons per day. In England, teachers are delivering an average of six lessons per day, and this adds up to 960 hours per year. This means that a Finnish teacher has over 300 more hours per year to work with their peers and collaborate than their UK equivalent. Lesson planning, developing the curriculum and bouncing new ideas around are all deeply embedded in the Finnish model. Non-teaching blocks are typically scheduled with another teacher in a Finnish school, meaning it's rarer to be working alone that it is with a colleague. Likewise, it is typical to have in-class support from one of your peers two or three times per week. This isn't with support staff or teaching assistants. It is with a fully accredited teacher. This is the foundation of how they drive their exception results. Fresh perspectives, new insights and friendly colleagues are easily undervalued in an overwhelming environment that demands test results and targets, but these are the things that make the difference.

Schools in the UK are not about to drop two classes from their daily timetable to match Finland, but there are other ways that teachers can collaborate, despite their time restrictions. Technology can fill the gap, and cloud platforms make it effortless. Through apps such as Google Docs, teachers can work together virtually as if they are sat in the same room. This kind of collaboration is essential within a school because the collective knowledge of a group is always greater than the individual knowledge of even the most brilliant of teachers. This is what Parkroyal achieved through the use of G Suite; a little bit of Finland in the heart of Crewe.

Creating Personalised Learning

TRUE PERSONALISED LEARNING requires sophisticated data and analysis systems. Every day, teachers at

Parkroyal Community Primary School login to their assessment system and have access to live data, with insight and analysis into their students' performance from as recently as the previous lesson. Once staff have captured and recorded data, their technology assesses and analyses the results to identify trends, patterns and weaknesses. Many schools rely on outdated assessment systems that are little more than glorified spreadsheets. They record data, but any analysis is still reliant on a member of staff. At Parkroyal this is a thing of the past and it is transforming how learning takes place for students at the school. Personalised learning is now a reality and the school's leadership have the ability to implement new initiatives and react to challenges with just days' notice.

The new generation of education assessment and student management systems use real time insights and automated analytics, thereby removing the need for teachers to wade through reams of data to try to make sense of it, and providing the school with the information they need to personalise learning in an instant.

I could walk into Parkroyal tomorrow, and within sixty seconds anyone with access to their assessment system could show me student progress right up to that day. Leaders can identify students that are falling behind within just a few lessons. The average primary school would take weeks to do the same, and dozens of lessons would have passed by. This kind of insight enables Parkroyal to do everything within their power to stop students from falling behind. This is an important point because this makes student progress at Parkroyal proactive. The average school is reactive. This is not a criticism, but a reflection of the assessment and student data systems that the average schools rely on. Even some of the most established school software systems on the market aren't able to analyse data and highlight trends to the extent that the new generation of systems can. It's a simple limitation of the technology that sits behind these older assessment systems, many of which were developed well over ten years ago now.

In a classroom of thirty students, one of the biggest challenges for any teacher is to identify who requires specialised support. Often students will sit quietly rather than ask for help even if they haven't grasped the learning. Teachers can develop great intuition, but this isn't something that develops overnight and can take years of practice. This is where leadership must support teachers to identify student needs much earlier. Prior to using Cloud technology, teachers at Parkroyal had to wait anywhere between four to eight weeks for an assessment cycle to be completed. Today, there is real no comparison: they are able to monitor student progress on a daily basis if they choose, and without introducing any additional testing or marking.

If you want to know whether your data management system is up to date, see if you can answer the following question: "How many of your English as a second language students, who qualify for free school meals and have an attendance of below 80% are making the expected progress across English and maths?" Using your existing student data and assessment systems could you give me an answer within sixty seconds? Or would it take someone hours, or even days sat down looking through reams of spreadsheets to work it out? I'd suspect that it'd be the latter and if that is the case you need to change your system. Many schools rely on systems that 'silo' data, storing it in separate systems that don't integrate with one another. The assessment system is separate from the attendance system, which is separate from the finance system. This makes it difficult, if not impossible, to identify trends, and if you can't easily identify trends you can't easily react to them. It is impossible to truly personalise learning under this system, and with that you reduce the capability of your teachers.

Many schools don't want to face up to the fact that their systems are underpowered, which in itself I find a little strange. I've met headteachers who will tell me, "Well, we don't really need to know that information, all we need to know is whether students are getting the results they should." But schools do need to know this kind of information. Our education system, rightly or wrongly, is moving towards an value-added model and schools are being asked to demonstrate how spending impacts on student progress.

With the right school systems in place you can pinpoint which students need additional help, and which initiatives are going to best provide it to them. That is true personalised learning.

Making assessment quicker

I WANT TO take you to another school that has benefitted from cloud technology. In 2014, we delivered a project with Broadgreen International School. The goal was to turn around an underperforming maths department at key stage three. Having assessed the department and sat down with the school's leadership team, I focused on one key area: the development of their assessment system. At the start of the project it took two weeks for a teacher to complete a full marking cycle. By the end of the project we had reduced this to forty-eight hours (with some teachers marking as quickly as twenty-four hours). The impact for students was remarkable, and independent learning increased by 97% within just five weeks. Between 2014 and 2015, students achieving the expected level of progress in maths rose from 41% to 51%.

What was most interesting is that when we surveyed the students, they talked about how much more enjoyable and engaging maths lessons were under the new assessment system.

2-week marking cycle: 50%   2-day marking cycle: 84%

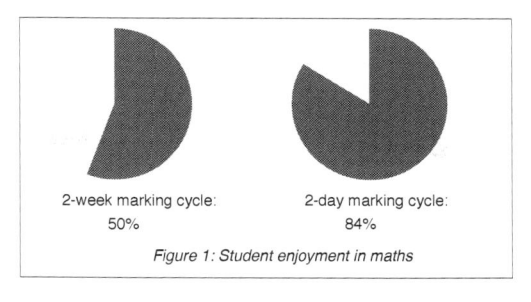

Figure 1: Student enjoyment in maths

At the beginning of the project, 56% of students rated their enjoyment in the subject as excellent or good. By the end of the project, that number had risen to 84%. What was most interesting is that our work on the project didn't focus on classroom content, yet students were reporting that lessons were significantly more enjoyable and engaging. This flies in the face of the perceived wisdom in education that to improve a subject you focus on the development of the curriculum and available teaching resources. Our philosophy was simple. First, teachers are passionate and experienced in their field, and they should be trusted with the development of their students. Second, if teachers have better access to student progress data and have available time, they will pour their passion and experience into their students who need it most. All we did was to give teachers the tools they needed and freed up time for them to develop more outstanding learning opportunities in their maths lessons. The rest took care of itself.

It is easy to develop a myopic view that every school initiative must revolve around students. In order to meet the students' needs, however, I believe that initiatives must revolve around teachers, because no schools has ever been better than its teachers. To borrow a phrase from Richard Branson, the billionaire serial entrepreneur, "Clients do not come first. Employees come first. If you take care of your employees, they will take care of your clients". Take care of your teachers, and they will take care of your students.

When it comes to the use of technology, if you truly want to improve student progress, then focus technology on improving the capability of your teachers. Empowering them to be more effective, freeing up their time and to giving them the insights they crave are all easily achievable through technology. If you can do that, so long as you have the right teachers in your school, then the rest will take care of itself and school improvement will be a lot easier than you imagined.

Key Takeaways

- Embrace cloud technology to make learning resources and student data available to teachers whenever and wherever they need it.
- Focus new technology initiatives to benefit teachers first. If you look after your teachers, they will look after your students.
- Employ technology to do the heavy lifting when it comes to administration. When teachers spend less time on paperwork they can spend more time on students.

CHAPTER 4

Principle One: Improving the Capability of your Team (Part 2)

"Teamwork is the ability to work together toward a common vision. The ability to direct individual accomplishments toward organisational objectives. It is the fuel that allows common people to attain uncommon results."

Andrew Carnegie

Jack was having a tough day. A month had gone by, and the only applicants he'd received for the science teacher role were all fresh out of University. Jack was the assistant head in a large secondary school that was deemed to be underperforming, and for the third year in a row the school was experiencing a 'brain drain', as it's best and most experienced teachers moved on. With two better performing secondary schools just a few miles down the road in each direction, Jack's school was struggling to compete for the best applicants and the ratio in key departments had shifted significantly towards younger, less experienced staff. With budget cuts on the horizon, Jack struggled to see how the situation was going to get any better.

The story of Jack is by no means unique, and many schools across the country are finding it increasingly difficult to hire the calibre of staff they seek. With The Department of Education experiencing challenges in both recruiting and retaining teachers, and an additional one million school places needed by 2023, all signs indicate that schools will find themselves in a highly competitive environment when hiring new staff. This will make it all the more important to focus on how you improve the capability of your current team as bringing in A-grade teachers as a means to improve school performance may become a thing of the past.

In this chapter, I will explain why schools that work better as a team achieve much more and the role that technology plays in this. I'll look at the two key concepts of communication and collaboration, and how by developing each of these will help you to create invested, empowered staff that will significantly outperform the sum of their parts.

Listening to your teachers

HOW OFTEN DO you listen to your classroom teachers and their concerns about the school? Who do you know in the staffroom that asks for help with the areas of their job they find most difficult? How much constructive criticism is fed up the chain of command, and how often is it taken seriously and acted upon?

I've asked this question in many schools over the years and I'm often met with a blank stare. In the previous chapter, I touched on the concept that in the development of your school initiatives should revolve around teachers rather than students. The better your teachers are able to perform, the better your students will perform. Therefore the question on every school leader's lips shouldn't be "How do we improve student performance?" It should be "How do we improve teacher performance?" and the easiest way to start is by listening to them.

You may feel confident that you already listen to your staff. There are weekly meetings, the annual staff survey and regular performance meetings within teams that all offer teachers the opportunity to voice their opinions. Yet, if we want to galvanise whole school support and drive performance upwards, these current arrangements do little more than pay lip service to that goal. The reason is quite simple. The age old problem of 'us vs them'. As a school leadership team, the power balance through these social situations is inextricably weighted in your favour. Weekly meetings are lead by a senior leader, staff surveys are rarely acted upon and performance meetings are always one sided. Are you truly listening to your teachers or are you creating social situations where they have no option but to conform to the ideals you have already laid out?

This is not about handing over the keys to the crown jewels, but in empowering every teacher in your school to improve the whole organisation. The technological aspect of implementing this is straightforward.

By using cloud technology you can create a live school handbook, complete with goals, vision and policies. Online collaboration functions allow staff to comment and suggest revisions to policies, or better yet to debate these online. For many school leaders, twenty-two teachers discussing the merits of their current assessment system is probably their idea of a nightmare. However, once you get over the initial shock of relinquishing that control you'll find that those debates reveal nuggets of gold. Teachers will find small ways to improve aspects across the school each week. I can't state how powerful this information is, because this is teachers telling you, the leadership team, exactly how you can improve the learning environment in the classrooms. In the grand scheme of your school's development, opening policies for debate may feel like a solitary raindrop in the midst of a thunderstorm, but even the smallest of things can make a significant impact. By using technology to open up school policies for debate, you empower teachers to take ownership of the school's development and improvement.

When LearnMaker worked with Invicta Primary School in 2016, I made sure to incorporate as much staff engagement into the ongoing development of the school as possible. Today, Invicta has a live staff handbook that everyone in the school can access via G Suite. School leaders have reported that staff take more responsibility in their roles now, as all rules and regulations are transparent across the school. Staff are beginning to provide feedback on school policies and better shape the school's future progress. No one knows the classroom environment better than the teachers who work in it, and the feedback Invicta's teachers provide is enabling the leadership team to better target areas of opportunity and develop more rapidly. What's more, new staff joining the school are up and running within a matter of weeks. Prior to using cloud technology, it would take a new teacher months to adapt to the ways of working that are unique to Invicta Primary School. Today that is a thing of the past.

Achieving more with empowered, invested teams

ONCE TEACHERS ARE engaged, you can then begin to empower them. If you can better empower teachers, then as long as they're passionate and knowledgeable, they will do the rest and school improvement will become a lot more straightforward than you imagined.

Empowerment comes on two levels. Teachers need to understand exactly what they can and can't do. This sounds like common sense, but in many schools policies and staff handbooks are not readily available. In the past few weeks, I've visited schools and each one had their own unique way of approaching this. The first school I visited had over one hundred policies stored on the school server. The headteacher had kept every policy they had created for over ten years, yet they weren't organised by year, by field or in any meaningful way. The result was that staff didn't know what was current and what wasn't, so people relied on being told what to do instead of finding out for themselves. It had created a state of inertia throughout the school. The headteacher told me of the leadership team's struggles in launching new initiatives. Staff simply wouldn't put new ideas into practice until the leadership team bore down on them, and even then, many would return with questions and concerns that had already been covered in meetings. Staff literally needed to be dragged on any journey that the school wanted to take. When I spent time with the staff and ran an anonymous survey, the same theme kept coming up. Staff were unsure and confused about what they could and couldn't do, and from their point of view the leadership team embarked on new initiatives seemingly overnight. They were because they were confused by the lack of transparency that the leadership team had created. The most surprising part of the whole visit was this wasn't some underperforming or failing school, as you might expect that; it was rated outstanding.

A week later, I visited another school that was the polar opposite. This school had trimmed their policies down to twenty seven and kept them stored in a filing cabinet located in the headteacher's office. It was a small school and they operated an 'open door' policy that encouraged teachers to knock on the head's door at any time of day. Yet the same problems around inertia existed in this school too, and few, if any of the staff had ever looked at the school policies. In this school checking the policies meant interrupting the headteacher, and no matter how cordial and friendly they may be no one wants to be interrupting their boss multiple times a week. It's a work faux par. Just like the first school, teachers here waited for instructions before taking action. This time is was physical barriers that had reduced school transparency.

solution of both of these schools is to develop a cloud-based digital handbook in which all school policies can be found. Policies are little more than guidelines and rules to achieve a set of desired outcomes. They should not be set in stone. Once they become inflexible, they limit how much your school can improve. I've put this concept into practice first-hand with many of the schools I've worked with, and it never ceases to amaze me the impact it can have. By helping schools empower their teachers I've seen them save time, save money and improve learning opportunities. Education is filled with consultants who charge exorbitant sums of money to come in and do this type of work for your school. Simply empower your teachers to do the same. It might surprise you how well they know the school and what is needed to move it forward.

Increasing the capability of your support staff

THE BEST PERFORMING schools spend a lower percentage of their budget on support staff than their lower performing peers. A study of UK secondary schools found that the top performing 20% spent £300 less per pupil than the bottom 20% of schools. That is a significant finding, and scaled up over a whole school it would give an average sized secondary an additional £240,000 per year in their budget. The study found that the poorest performing schools were deploying support staff in more general roles, such as general classroom or teaching assistants. The higher performing schools were utilising support staff in more specialist ways, focusing on reducing the administrative and workload burdens of teachers.

St Peter's High School in Manchester is an average sized secondary school in an area of significant deprivation. 48% of pupils are eligible for free school meals and 70% have been eligible for free school meals at some point in the last six years. 44% of pupils speak English as a second language and there are 64 different first languages spoken. The school was rated outstanding by Ofsted in 2009, and they've seen first-hand the beneficial impact of investing in support staff for very clearly defined roles. Seven support staff, led by an experienced teacher, are employed within a study room environment to accelerate learning and provide academic support. The school recruits recent graduates who are considering a career in teaching. This has allowed teachers to concentrate on teaching within the classroom while support staff are empowered and trained to focus on individualised learning, often with vulnerable pupils.

The barrier to this strategy is a lack of technology to support staff redeployment. For most schools, there is no way to work collaboratively that doesn't involve sitting around a table. When teachers have just a handful of free periods over a school week, there is too little time for them to sit down and work with support staff, so schools go back to the only option they have: placing support staff in the lesson. With cloud technology, however, you can save time planning lessons and use the time to work together with support staff.

In the previous chapter, I looked at how you go about improving the capability of individual teachers through more effective collaboration. What you'll see throughout this book is that each of the principles are interlinked, and the same methods that can improve collaboration between teachers can improve collaboration between teachers and support staff. Cloud platforms enable you to begin putting this into practice right now at no cost. Once teams of teachers and support staff can better work together, you'll find that you can easily replicate the results that St Peter's High School are seeing in your own school.

Key Takeaways

- Empowering teachers and support staff to work more closely together through cloud technology will improve their effectiveness while also reducing staffing costs.
- Leveraging the knowledge and insights of your teachers by opening school policies for revision is a cost effective and powerful school development strategy.
- Using technology to give teachers a voice in your school's development will only improve their commitment and passion in their role

CHAPTER 5

Principle Two: Improving the Productivity of Schools

"Productivity is never an accident. It is always the result of a commitment to excellence, intelligent planning, and focused effort."
                                    Paul J. Meyer

Helen is head of the English department and deputy head in a larger than average secondary school. Each week Helen arrives at her desk in school at 7.30am. She eats a quick breakfast and gets in an hour of work before making her way over to the staff room for the morning briefing. After teaching four lessons, planning work for the next module, overviewing the department's progress and having meetings with the headteacher, Helen leaves for home just after 5pm. On the back seat of her car sit 50-100 exercise books that Helen will mark that night. After a short dinner with her partner and children, Helen sits down in front of the TV and begins tackling the pile of books. Sometime, usually around 8pm, Helen will place the last exercise book down and open her email. She'll sort through the 50 emails she's received that day, many of which she didn't need to be copied into, and at 9pm she'll be done for the evening. Helen will do this around 150 times per year.

I opened this book with the figure of one billion pound: this is the amount that has been spent on technology by UK schools in the last five years, and all to no effect. This statistic does not come as a surprise to me. I'm afraid that everything I have seen within schools tells me that most are poor at budgeting. Money is poured into projects without adequate planning, and technical and implementation problems are patched over with short-term solutions that cost significantly more down the line. The same is true of productivity. UK schools tend to rely on inefficient systems that waste time and put enormous pressure on teachers to perform all of their duties to time. These habits are so entrenched that, for many, it is unthinkable that there is any other way. Meetings, non-stop photocopying and data capture are carried out with a sense of inevitability: this is the way it has always been done, and this is the way all schools do it! Before you accept this as an inevitable truth, it is worth looking to your peers. A 2016 study by the Education Policy Institute (EPI) found that teachers in the UK work the most hours of any European country, and to what end? There is no research that suggests longer working hours for teachers equates to better teaching and learning. It is a sign of inefficiency. I want to be clear that this is about the inefficiency of systems, not individuals, many of whom are desperate to focus on their passion for teaching rather than spending endless hours on admin and paperwork.

When I suggest to headteachers that they should focus on productivity to improve teaching and learning, I am commonly met with the response that greater productivity is not a priority, nor relevant to their overarching learning goals. I feel that this attitude misses the point, because while it is easy to point to a need for structural reform across UK education to meet modern challenges, it sidelines the debate about how we can improve the quality of our schools and the lives of our teachers right now.

If you focus on a target like improving attainment of A-C grades in GCSE English, but have an English department that is already working overtime and is at the limit of its allocated budget, then this limits what progress you can make. I see this all the time in my travels up and down the UK. Schools aim for better learning outcomes but without addressing the long-standing issues that stymie the functioning of the school. This can be anything from WiFi that doesn't work to technology the staff can't use. To make long-lasting change, you must improve the educational environment of your school holistically, and that means looking at the needs of your teachers and senior leaders first.

Moreover, poor productivity is not benign. It is harmful to the functioning of any organisation. It is not good enough to say 'Well, it's not perfect but it will do.' if your school is unproductive then, compared to a more efficient school down the road, it will spend more money and its staff will have to work harder and longer to achieve the same results. This means it will be slower to react to external changes from the Department of Education and Ofsted, and in all likelihood, your staff will be under more stress, become unmotivated and eventually leave (often to the better performing school down the road!)

This chapter explains why schools that get more done for less are able to offer a better education to students, and how schools can use technology to save significant amounts of time and money. I will draw on the projects LearnMaker carried out to improve productivity with Invicta Primary School, Broadgreen International School and Parkroyal Community Primary School, and demonstrate how this has transformed learning in each.

How to Save Time

TO SAVE TIME, schools must look at their systems and processes and ask themselves how they can simplify basic tasks. Technology can provide a wealth of solutions to some of the biggest problems that teachers tell me about (too much to do, not enough time – does that ring a bell?) and can influence your work environment in ways that would have been unthinkable a decade ago. However, technology must be bought with these aims in mind and implemented properly, or it will become part of the problem.

Here is a simple rundown of how cloud software can save your school time.

1. Reduce how much admin takes place

Patrick Bambrick-Santoyo, an applauded school leader and founder of the Leverage Leadership Institute, found that school leaders spend 50% of their time on administration and operational issues and only 6% on improving the quality of classroom instruction. This data relates to American schools, but I have no doubt that this statistic would be at least as bad for UK schools. I have seen firsthand how many admin tasks fill up headteachers' time and the inertia this creates. If a school leader can't find the time to lead, there is no chance of the school's staff and students reaching their potential.

Paperwork bogs down staff at every level of school, yet it is across the administration teams I see schools struggling the most. If your office team aren't productive, then there is no hope for anyone else in your school, because admin sits at the heart of the organisation.

Reduce the amount of paperwork for one member of staff and you'll see a knock-on effect across the school. This was certainly the case at Parkroyal, with whom I worked in 2015. Before the start of the project, the headteacher's talented and highly-skilled PA spent most of her time performing basic admin duties. One of these was to record incidents. If a child got a bruise from a fall in the playground, for example, she would type up the pink incident slip as it arrived at the office into the school system and write a slip informing parents. If the incident was urgent, she would inform the headteacher. As they had no shared calendar, this would sometimes involve asking around until someone could point her in the right direction. A single incident could take anywhere up to thirty minutes to complete. This process, repeated multiple times in a week, was taking up hours of her time.

These manual, people intensive processes should be a thing of the past, yet they plague schools across the country. When Parkroyal approached me to look at how they could use technology to drive school performance, automation was one of the first things I identified. We implemented G Suite which enabled staff across the school to communicate quickly and easily. It makes tasks like incident reporting infinitely faster. Today at Parkroyal, if a child takes a fall in the playground, the attending teacher fills out an online form on their tablet device. This instantly populates a spreadsheet that both the PA and headteacher have access to. Parkroyal had recently updated their student management system which we've already touched on in the previous chapter. The online form Parkroyal use is integrated with their student management system, and it automatically generates a text to inform parents of the incident. No more pink slips sat on the desk. No more low level administration work for the PA; now they have a system that utilises technology in order to save time and reduce administration work.

When running a school, it can be difficult to find time to focus on seemingly small issues like this, but how well these individual cogs run in the development of your whole school is critical. On one occasion, a serious incident took place at Parkroyal that required an emergency service to be called. With cloud technology in place, the headteacher knew of what had happened within sixty seconds and was able to respond immediately.

Another big drain for the PA at Parkroyal was assessment data entry. In other words, manually entering long lists of students' marks onto the system for them to be analysed at a later date. Having moved to a new generation of school assessment systems, this is a thing of the past. Teachers upload marks from their own device, and their new system analyses the data automatically and maps trends from which the school leadership can make decisions.

Freed from the bane of data entry, the PA now has the opportunity to put her talent to better use. Since the project with Parkroyal, she has been able to dedicate her time to vetting new recruits for the school and explore commercial opportunities to find more money for the school. Both of these jobs previously fell to the headteacher, who is now able to spend more of time focused on improving learning outcomes. This demonstrates the knock-on effect I described earlier; not only is the PA's time put to better use, but, crucially, Parkroyal's head is also spending less time on admin and has more hours available in a week to dedicate to leadership.

2. Reduce how long you spend marking

Yep, teachers hate marking. There are probably more delicate ways to state this, but why bother? Marking is one of the most time-consuming parts of teaching and few teachers would shed tears if it was done away with altogether. This extract from a Guardian article entitled 'Six Teachers on a Typical Workday' is typical of a teacher's experience in the UK:

I'm a head of department in a state school in London and my average day is as follows:

Arrive to school 8am

Leave school 6.30 / 7pm (later if there's a parents evening or open evening)

2hrs of planning / e-mails / marking taken home at least 3 nights per week.

3/4 hours planning or marking on a Sunday.
Working week = 62 hrs per week.

Guardian - 2nd April 2013

In the previous chapter, I mentioned my work with Broadgreen International School and their assessment process. It was not unusual for the maths teachers at the school to take home 100 books a night, three nights a week. Before our work with them, it took a teacher two weeks to complete a full marking cycle. Students handed work in, their teacher gave initial feedback, students responded and the teacher gave their final comments. Over that two week period, students would only have three structured interactions with their teacher in regards to their work.

I was quite astounded by the inefficiency of this process so I introduced the maths department to a cloud based digital assessment platform available through any web browser and as an app (on selected devices). This technology digitises marking, allowing teachers to provide written annotations, audio and video feedback, along with interacting with students via the instant messaging function.

Within five weeks of the project, the department had transitioned over to digital assessment. The two week marking cycle had been reduced to forty-eight hours. In this time, teachers would interact with students an average of nine times, a 300% increase on the three interactions on the paper-based assessment cycle. Not only did the technology save teachers time, but it improved the level and depth of interaction they were able to have with students.

If it is hard to imagine how one simple piece of technology can save so much time, then here is just one example of how it made light work of so much marking. Year 8 students had just begun learning algebra for the first time and it was the first module where teachers would be solely using digital assessment to mark homework. Mark, the Head of Department, identified a trend: about 60% of his students were making the same mistake on their working out. He filmed a short video solving the equation using the correct technique and narrated the steps he took. He then sent the video out to all the students who needed it. As he was using a digital, cloud based platform, Mark was able to send the video to over sixty students with just a few clicks. It took less than five minutes to film, narrate and send the video to his students. As each student has their own login and folder, all feedback was saved and accessible at any time. Had Mark still been marking on paper he would have needed to comment and correct sixty exercise books. Hours of work, rather than minutes.

As I already covered under Principle One, digital assessment did more than save the maths department time. Although not the sole reason, it contributed significantly towards the rise in A-C grade GCSE results from 41% to 51% in one year. This is clear evidence to me that productivity is more than just an issue of time and money. It is about freeing up your teachers so that they can perform to the best of their ability. If you want your teachers to reach their potential, then you must have the systems in place to support that. If you don't, all your efforts towards this aim will be futile.

Broadgreen's head of maths also saved substantial departmental time. Each term, Mark would need to invigilate all teacher feedback in the department to ensure it was up to the standard that was expected. Before digital assessment was introduced, this meant Mark would need to sift through dozens of exercise books from each of the seven teachers in the department. Today, Mark has live access to his teacher's feedback. Instead of undertaking one large book trawl at the end of the term, Mark is able to check on the quality of marking on a weekly basis, providing feedback and support to teachers and further nudging the department's performance upwards.

3. Reduce how many meetings you have

A teacher, regardless of her role, should not sit through more than one hour of internal meetings per week. Any more than that is a reflection of how unproductive a school has become. I know of a senior school leader who spent over five hours a week in meetings. These all took place after hours, and ate significantly into what little personal life she had. The assumption was that there was no way around them. How else would she be up to date on student performance, strategic updates or hear what was happening at the classroom level in her department?

The trouble for most schools is that they currently have no other way to complete vital tasks. Senior leaders are required to collaborate on documents relating to issues like policy, strategic goals and curriculum development, and this means sitting together in a room to discuss the document in question. Senior leaders might meet multiple times just to create one document, even if it is done sequentially (one teacher must wait for the input of another before offering their own).

Technology has improved so significantly, that it's actually possible to avoid having all but a few meetings. Since working with LearnMaker, Parkroyal School now uses G Suite to share working documents with multiple people simultaneously. Instead of meeting around a table, each teacher can access the document and add their input at any time, from anywhere. As a result, the hour-long leadership meetings on a Tuesday evening are a thing of the past at Parkroyal. It's important to note that removing the leadership meeting from the schedule didn't save the school one hour. It saved an hour for every staff member present. In a year, that's a significant amount of time saved for a school. Beforehand, the meeting was the only way for senior leaders to be kept up to date on strategic goals. Now this information is available through G Suite in real time. Not only has the school saved time, but G Suites collaboration and communications functions mean the leadership team is able to implement strategies throughout the school much faster.

There are other ways that cloud technology can simplify the way you work. It saved one executive headteacher three hours from her working week. Marie, executive head of Invicta Primary, used to spend hours each week attending meetings between Invicta's two sites. A lot of this time was spent in her car driving the three miles through London traffic. On a good day the journey might take twenty minutes but on a bad day it could take forty-five. After our project, Marie now uses video conferencing software to hold virtual meetings, allowing her to get down to business without wasting time stuck in traffic.

Improve how your team communicates

WHEN I JOINED the corporate team at Apple, I went through their renowned in-house training. In my first year with the company I must have spent at least ten full days in training sessions learning how to best communicate. That may seem excessive, after all most of us are able to string a sentence together, but this attention to detail is what separates Apple from its competition. Apple understands that communication is at the heart of all high performance. Without good communication, you are simply lost, and what I learned with them has always stayed with me. I was taught:

- If it needs to be done within the next 30 minutes, pick up the phone
- If it needs to be done today, then instant message
- If it needs to be done in a couple of days, then email

I was also taught that if an email needs to be acted upon, then it should convey one point only. This is best practice to ensure people know what is expected of them and don't need to email back to ask for clarification.

To save time and streamline communication, schools should look to harness the benefits of the tools that cloud platforms offer. Working with Invicta Primary in 2015, we helped them to do exactly that. Before the project began, executive head Marie would regularly need to sort through around a hundred emails every single night after work. Most didn't require her direct input, and had her cc'd in to 'keep her in the loop' of developments. This happens in a lot for people at the top of organisations, not just schools, and it's a real time killer. By diving into Invicta's email system, we could see that each month about 12,000 emails were being sent internally between a staff of under a hundred. This was happening because there was no other way of communicating. Invicta, like the majority of schools, lacked the systems to ease the burden of email. Once they had moved to a cloud platform, the school began to use its instant messaging system, and within fifteen weeks, the amount of internal emails reduced by half. 12,000 per month down to 6000 per month. As time goes by that number continues to fall and staff are communicating more frequently and at a much faster rate.

If you have the right tools in place, you can use the following flowchart to decide the best means to communicate and avoid unnecessary meetings and email chains:

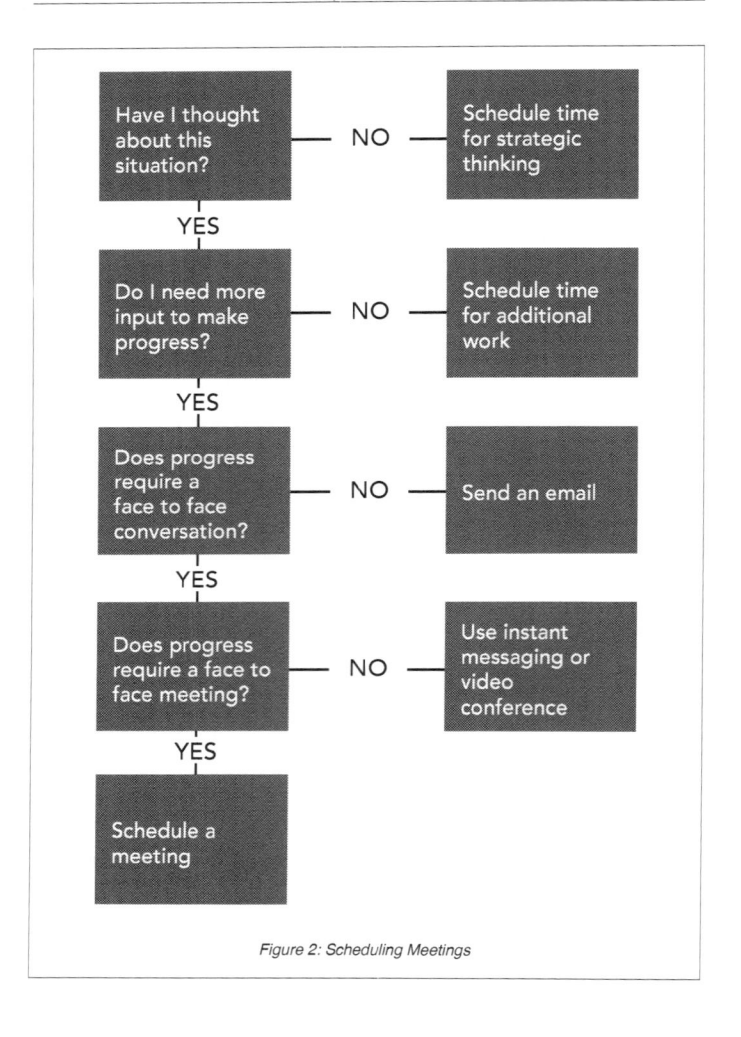

```
┌─────────────────┐       ┌─────────────────┐
│ Have I thought  │       │ Schedule time   │
│ about this      │— NO —│ for strategic   │
│ situation?      │       │ thinking        │
└─────────────────┘       └─────────────────┘
         │
        YES
         │
┌─────────────────┐       ┌─────────────────┐
│ Do I need more  │       │ Schedule time   │
│ input to make   │— NO —│ for additional  │
│ progress?       │       │ work            │
└─────────────────┘       └─────────────────┘
         │
        YES
         │
┌─────────────────┐       ┌─────────────────┐
│ Does progress   │       │                 │
│ require a       │— NO —│ Send an email   │
│ face to face    │       │                 │
│ conversation?   │       │                 │
└─────────────────┘       └─────────────────┘
         │
        YES
         │
┌─────────────────┐       ┌─────────────────┐
│ Does progress   │       │ Use instant     │
│ require a face  │— NO —│ messaging or    │
│ to face meeting?│       │ video           │
│                 │       │ conference      │
└─────────────────┘       └─────────────────┘
         │
        YES
         │
┌─────────────────┐
│ Schedule a      │
│ meeting         │
└─────────────────┘
```

Figure 2: Scheduling Meetings

If your school's answer to all of the questions in the flowchart is to 'have a meeting', then you aren't putting your time, money and talent to best use.

Reduce how long you spend assessing data

I WANT TO revisit the acid test I set schools from the previous chapter. Here's a question for you: how many of your English as a second language students who qualify for free school meals with an attendance of below 80% are making the expected progress across English and maths? In the Capability chapter I explored how underpowered many school's data and assessment systems are.

The problem occurs because schools still rely on manual systems that take weeks to produce output. This means that you only get a superficial glimpse of student progress. I recommend schools stick to one rule when it comes to data assessment: if the system requires human input after the first assessment point, then it's too slow. Book trawls are the perfect example of this. This is how it is done in almost every school I meet:

```
┌─────────────────────────────────────┐
│   Teachers marks student's works    │
└─────────────────────────────────────┘
                  ↓
┌─────────────────────────────────────┐
│  Teachers collates and evaluates    │
│  students' work at the end of an    │
│         assessment cycle            │
└─────────────────────────────────────┘
                  ↓
┌─────────────────────────────────────┐
│ Senior leaders collate assessment   │
│ cycle data and upload it into       │
│         assessment system           │
└─────────────────────────────────────┘
                  ↓
┌─────────────────────────────────────┐
│ Senior leaders analyse assessment   │
│    data and plot against targets    │
└─────────────────────────────────────┘
                  ↓
┌─────────────────────────────────────┐
│ Leadership team identifies where    │
│ improvements are needed and organize│
│            interventions            │
└─────────────────────────────────────┘
```

Figure 3: Assessing Data

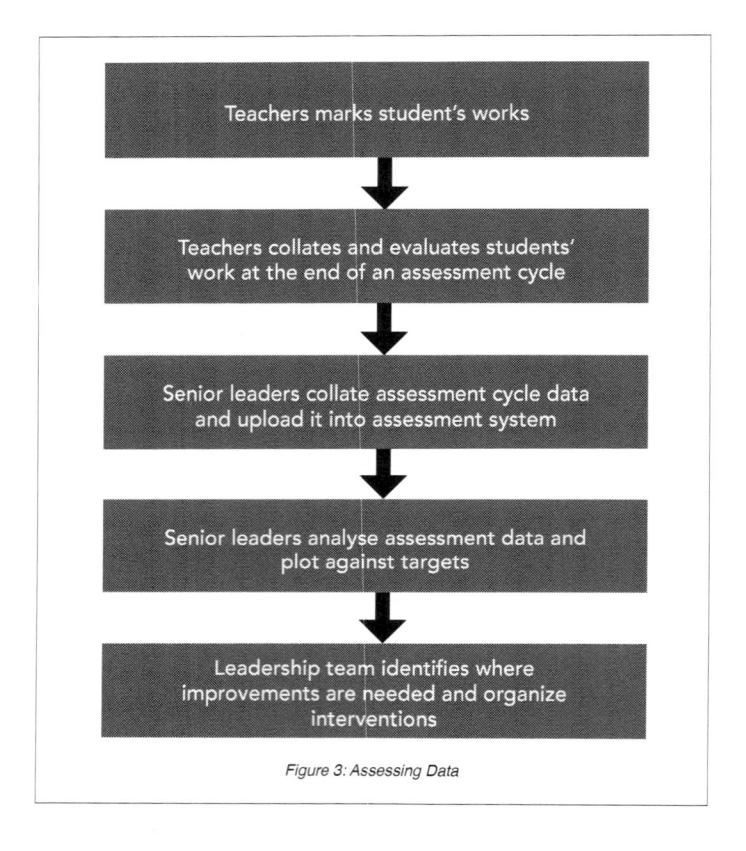

This is a poor system by any standards. By the time interventions and support have reached the students who need it, almost three months will have gone by. Let's imagine that a student begins falling behind in a subject. It will take about sixty days before the leadership team gains awareness of this and about another thirty days before it reaches the student in question. If the student has fallen behind in a core subject then they've sat through anywhere between forty-eight to sixty lessons, depending on the timetable, before support reaches them. This is why students getting E and D grades don't turn them into Bs or As. Too much time has been lost.

Instead, technology must be engaged at the first point of assessment. When I worked with Parkroyal in 2014, the focus was on how we could best use their new assessment system and cloud platform to provide this opportunity. As a result, this is how Parkroyal carry out the same process:

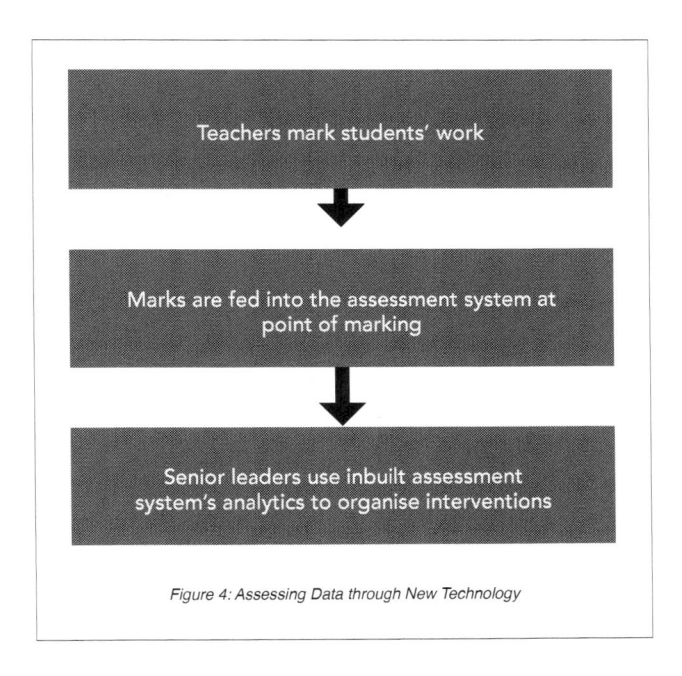

```
Teachers mark students' work
        ↓
Marks are fed into the assessment system at
point of marking
        ↓
Senior leaders use inbuilt assessment
system's analytics to organise interventions
```

Figure 4: Assessing Data through New Technology

Senior leadership team use their assessment system's analytics to personalise learning as and when it needs to

I've long been a huge fan of the work of Sir Ken Robinson and his insight into standardised schooling's failure to enable children to fully explore themselves or find their passions. This is not a critique of the individuals in education, but of the systems that are imposed onto it by politics. I see Robinson's philosophy reflected in my own career path. I excelled academically and was a straight-A student, but after leaving school I struggled to settle on something that made me happy. I went to University, I became a musician, taught in schools, worked at Apple, became a trainer, went into sales and then finally, in the summer of 2014, I realised my own passions: education, technology and improving performance. Within two months I'd quit my career and started LearnMaker. I realise that I'm lucky in that I'm not afraid to take risks. I'm filled with optimism for the future and believe we can shape our own destiny. However, I'm also a pragmatist. Robinson paints a fantastic vision for what organised schooling could be, but he offers no roadmap for how we get there. This is where I see technology bridging the gap, and helping us forwards towards the Robinson philosophy of truly personalised learning. At Parkroyal, they are able to spot trends and identify learning opportunities for students that other schools simply can't because the technology takes care of all the analytics for them. Technology doesn't sleep, it works twenty-four hours a day, seven days a week, and Parkroyal use this advantage to personalise learning for their students like never before.

A note on evidencing

THE NEED TO evidence learning that has put a bigger strain on teachers and schools than anything else in the past few years.

Some schools have reached fanatical levels of detail when it comes to assessing students and evidencing the results. Nowhere is this better demonstrated than with the colour pen marking systems that has invaded primary schools everywhere. It's groupthink gone mad, and what started off in a handful of schools has become common practice across the country. Secondary schools are not exempt either, and it is commonplace that teachers are instructed by school leaders to write VF (which stands for 'verbal feedback given') on students' work whenever a conversation takes place.

There is enormous anxiety amongst senior staff in many schools that Ofsted will be unhappy if there isn't evidence of every student-teacher interaction that has taken place. The irony is that so much time is dedicated to gathering evidence that there is little left over to actually analyse the data this generates and better support learners. I have always worked on a ratio that I spend one minute looking at data and five minutes on implementation. I used this when I managed a staff of 100 at Apple and helped them to become one of the best performing teams in Europe.

When I joined Apple in 2010, my role was to work with the Dixons Group to improve the performance of the team to sell more Apple products. From my experience as a music teacher, I knew the importance of having robust assessment systems that would enable me to develop my team. On my first day in the role, I told my boss to expect mediocre results for the first three months while I built a system that would bring long-term success. By the end of the first quarter, I was right on track: I had some of the worst results in the country! By the third quarter, however, I'd become one of the best performers in the country, and within my first year, my store was in the top five performers in Europe. What separated me from my peers at Apple was that I had built a system that gave me daily performance updates. Every morning, the store manager and I would run a report on the previous day's staff performance. This was then uploaded into a dashboard I had built that tracked every member of staff's performance. This was built around the key performance indicators (KPIs) and helped me to identify opportunities and development needs in my team. This took about thirty minutes per morning, and I'd spend the rest of the day managing the team and working with individuals to develop them in the areas they needed most. By contrast, my peers at Apple waited for a weekly performance overview that didn't have anything like the same level of detail. Throughout my time at Apple, my store had the best conversion of customers to Apple Macs in Britain, and the methods I used to achieve this were developed into a full blown training programme for all new starters by the second year.

Real time analytics and assessment became standard in the commercial world years ago now, but schools still rely on outdated systems that take up far too much time and don't give senior leaders the information they need to make improvements. Until you have a live system in place, you will continue to miss learning opportunities for your students.

How to Save Money

MONEY IS WASTED in schools for two reasons: a lack of robust planning and spending on things that aren't needed. To save money, your school must (a) have a long-term strategy about how to implement what it spends on, whether this is technology or supply staff, and (b) re-evaluate the money it currently spends. Do you really need to spend tens of thousands of pounds on printing every year? Does all of that software you pay license fees for actually help teachers perform better?

Improving the productivity of a school is no one off exercise. It requires an ongoing commitment from the school's leadership, from the headteacher right up to the governors, to repeatedly identify and find new efficiencies within the school. Here are my solutions to some of the biggest drains on school budgets, to help you get started.

1. Create teaching resources collaboratively

There are many advantages to teachers working collaboratively, but here is one very concrete and measurable benefit: it will save you money. The case of Invicta Primary School is a great example of this. Before I started working with Invicta, the school was spending over £10,000 a year on printing. A conservative estimate is that since the project, the school has reduced printing by 33%, saving around £3000 per year. My strategy was to increase collaboration amongst staff using cloud technology, software that enables teachers to work together to create teaching resources (I discuss more of the benefits of this kind of collaboration in the Consistency chapter). In essence, teachers are now working together to create lesson resources across the curriculum, rather than relying on bought in lesson packs or downloadable worksheets. This was possible because G Suite allows teachers to work on the same document from any location. Better organisation has greatly reduced the need to print off so many worksheets and saved the school a small fortune.

It's difficult to pin down the exact amounts spent on printing across the UK education system, but a good rule of thumb to work to is that you're spend £100 per student each year. That means the average size primary spends the equivalent of a middle leaders salary on printing, while the average secondary spends two and a bit middle leaders salaries. With better systems in place, that money can be freed up to reinvest on something more worthwhile. Invicta have used it to bolster things like art supplies, rich classroom displays, exercise books and classroom stationery. All purchases to enrich the learning environment for children.

2. Spot the sharks in the water

St Mary's* Primary School left negotiations over their photocopier lease renewal feeling confident they had got a good deal: savings of £400 a year! Or so their supplier had led them to believe. In fact, the outstanding balance from the old contract was 'rolled over' and refinanced, compounding the interest and inflating the value of the lease. The contract was renewed for a fee of £18,500 and extended to five years. The school ended up paying £25,000 over this period, when they could have leased a copier with a different supplier for just over £4,000.

The plight of St Mary's, highlighted in The Department of Education's 2013 report Improving Efficiencies in Schools, is more common than you might think. There have been a number of examples recently of schools signing up to inappropriate photocopier deals that have cost between £25,000 and £200,000 over five year period.

Unfortunately, schools are easy pickings for shady sales people all too often. A lot of schools are still signed up to agreements made over ten years ago, and they're needlessly overpaying by thousands of pounds every month for key technology. Sometimes these agreements, for things like printers, don't even factor in the cost of ink or toners. A primary school I'm working with at the moment are spending £15,000 per on printer ink. It is very difficult for schools to negotiate well with suppliers because of the complexities of lease agreements and contract law, both of which the supplier is well versed in. There is no easy way around this. If you want to protect yourself against the sharks, you need someone with the right expertise in your team; typically, this means hiring a high quality School Business Manager. Negotiating deals and understanding contract law was never part of a teacher's job description, and this is precisely what unscrupulous suppliers take advantage.

3. Share the cost of a School Business Manager

Not all schools can afford to hire an experienced and high quality School Business Manager (SBM). This is a great pity, because a wide range of research has shown how great an impact SBMs have on improving productivity. The 2010 report, *'Cost Benefit Analysis of the School Business Management Programme',* by PricewaterhouseCoopers estimated that between 2002 and 2009, qualified SBMs generated £306m in savings for their schools. They also generated additional streams of income for schools and saved senior leaders time by reducing their workload.

The same year, research by Oakland Consulting found that for every £1 invested in a high quality SBM, they delivered savings of £11.67 in their first year. That means you're losing money by not employing one!

A high quality primary SBM will command a salary in excess of £45,000 per year, which is beyond the budgets of many schools. Just a few years ago, it would have been impossible for many smaller schools to get the benefit from this level of expertise, but technology has changed that. Cloud computing has removed geographical barriers to working relationships, and today a collective of small schools could easily share the cost of one high quality SBM between them. The SBM wouldn't even need to be onsite at particular schools, which broadens the options for whom you can team up with. Collaboration across schools is straightforward with cloud technology available. Shared documents, instant messaging and video conferencing are all free, making it easy to work across multiple sites and keep everyone up to date.

4. Ask other schools about their suppliers

If there is one thing that unscrupulous suppliers love to do, it's rip schools off. It's a scandal that there is so much variation in what schools pay for equipment, and yet there does not seem to be any great rush for anyone to do anything about it. This leaves schools in a terrible bind. The difference between what schools are charged for a single product can be over 1000%. Imagine that you paid £30,000 for a flatscreen TV and then found out that the school down the road paid £30 for the same item. I imagine you'd be reeling. Unbeknownst to many, this is exactly what is happening in schools across the UK. The problem of paying over the odds is highlighted in the Department of Education's Improving Efficiency in Schools (2013) which estimated that schools could collectively save one billion pound per year through smarter procurement and back office spending.

Avoiding this kind of waste is actually quite straightforward. It requires only that schools are willing to collaborate, and have the technology in place to link up with each other. Imagine your school set up a cloud-based database of suppliers to share with the local school cluster. Each school could add their supplier's details and their purchase prices.

Let's say your school is the first to buy tablets. You log the costs in the shared database. When the other twenty two schools come to buy tablets, they have a reference point for pricing from the database. They can contact the supplier directly, quoting the price they have, or they can try and get a better deal. If they get the better deal they then update the database and every other school benefits from it. This drives down costs. While you were buying tablets, another school purchased a set of new laptops, adding the details to the database. It comes time to buy some new laptops in your own school and voila, you have a reference point from which to start. It is this kind of practice, common in the business world, that would benefit schools so much and offer them protection from unscrupulous companies. The cloud platforms from which you could easily do this, are available right now.

The ATOS 100 Schools Data Collection Project sheds light on the extent of the problem with the lack of collaboration between schools. From a survey of three secondary and twenty primary schools, all based within fifteen miles of one another, they found that in one year the schools collectively used 1828 different suppliers. The schools were often paying a single supplier different amounts for the same products and services. If that wasn't bad enough, ATOS calculated that if each school spent thirty minutes meeting and setting their account up with just half of these suppliers, altogether this would have taken the twenty-three schools 27,420 hours of their time. If the schools had pooled their resources and worked collectively, the project estimates they could have saved 26,506 hours. That's 1152 hours per school, which is the same as having someone work thirty-six hours per week for a full school year.

5. *Spend more on training and less on technology*

Meadowbank Academy* invested £100,000 on 500 iPads for its students in 2014. It decided not to invest any money on training staff or implementation, confident that they could figure it out themselves. By 2016, the dream of putting technology in the hands of students had crumbled. The iPads seemed to be making teaching more complicated and teachers didn't feel confident using them. Those in charge reflected on the failure of the project and blamed the technology; it was too difficult to use and didn't seem to make lessons any better. The iPads were scrapped and the school spent another six figure sum on laptops to replace them. They chose not to invest in training or implementation. We can figure it out ourselves, they said once more.

There are many lessons to be learned from a school like Meadowbank. What hurt it the most was that senior leaders invested in a pile of iPads without any clear idea of what they were going to use them for. They didn't invest in training and implementation because they had no sense of what they wanted from the technology. As far as they were concerned, getting iPads into classrooms was the goal; the expectation was that the technology would just get to it and 'work'. Unfortunately, these kinds of purchases are extremely common in UK schools. Technology is bought without a clear plan of how it will be used or implemented, and sometimes with no intention of supporting staff to use them. It ends up costing schools eye-watering sums of money, either on repairing the damage the failed technology has done, or on replacing it with some other technology that may or may not make things better.

This reluctance to invest in training costs schools dearly. It would have cost Meadowbank about £10,000 to train staff adequately to use the iPads. Feeling reluctant to spend any more on them, they chose instead to buy entirely new technology, at a much greater cost. I think of this being a terrible poker player. You've got £100,000 bet in the hand (one game of poker) as you enter the final round. As the final card is turned another round of betting opens. Your opponent raises the stakes by £10,000. You're left with two options. To stay in the hand you must meet his bet or improve upon his bet. That means putting in at least another £10,000. If you can't, or don't want to meet his raise then you fold, and with it lose the £100,000 you've already bet. The hand is decided and one player wins it all. The cards are collected, a new hand is dealt and before you know it you're in for a fresh £100,000. This is exactly what schools like Meadowbank are doing when they scrap half-baked projects at the final round only to take the plunge into an equally costly and risky venture. The reality that schools need to confront is that teachers must have significant training and development to use classroom technology, and this means more than just brief, one-off workshops on how to use apps. Research by The Teachers Development Trust in 2014, suggests that teachers need a minimum of twenty-eight hours of development time to integrate one piece of learning into their daily practice. When you consider how many schools are reluctant to invest in training, it's easy to understand why all of this technology has had no impact on educational outcomes.

If you want technology in your school to improve performance, think about budgeting for training and implementation first, and technology second. The only way to mitigate and minimise risk is to dedicate time and effort to a clear and robust plan of action.

6. Don't buy things you don't need

I worked with a school that was spending £16,000 a year on software that sent parents an automated text message if their child wasn't marked in on the register. All this software did was to look at who was absent and fire off a text. The register software wasn't even supplied. The school was a large inner city secondary school, and for the same money, they could have hired a part-time admin assistant who could have performed the same job and fulfilled a whole host of other duties besides. I asked the school why they hadn't considered this much more cost-efficient option. They couldn't give me an answer.

Always ask yourself, 'why are we buying this?' before you commit to a purchase. Just because the technology exists does not mean your school needs it. Most schools I meet venture into expensive technology projects because a certain device is popular with other schools and because of a vague notion of 'improving engagement'. When pressed, I have found that many senior leaders struggle to explain what this means or how they expect the technology to impact upon it. Avoid this blasé attitude if you want you avoid making expensive errors of judgement.

Understand true value

IF YOU WANT to save money in the long-term, it is important to think wisely about how much you spend in the short-term. Spending more initially can save schools tens, if not hundreds of thousands of pounds later on. There are three simple rules in regards to true value you can stick to that will help you improve productivity:

1. Understand total cost of technology

Be aware of how much devices or software will cost beyond the initial price of the technology. Factor in things like license fees, maintenance and hardware lifespan in order to avoid budgeting disasters further down the line. Nobody is shocked to find that, once they have bought a car, they must also pay for petrol, road tax and insurance, yet it is not uncommon for people to be surprised by the running costs of technology. The assumption seems to be that the hardware should take care of itself. After all, technology is here to make our lives easier, right? The truth is that without careful planning it will almost certainly make your job more stressful and complicated. Think carefully about additional costs before you commit to a purchase.

2. Plan ahead and don't patch up problems

I worked with a large secondary school in Liverpool for a number of years. I had a great relationship with their resource manager and head of curriculum (they made me a bacon sandwich every time I turned up). Every six months, I'd get a call from them because a technical problem had rendered their devices useless. The IT manager was really out of his depth in this school and the problems that I was being called in for were the result of his inexperience. In the senior leaders' eyes, however, all the problems due to the antiquated school building not being up to the job. Everything would be better once they had their new build, they said. In 2015, they moved into a new building, and guess what, the problems not only continued, they increased! Once again, I was called in to come and help. This time, the school network wasn't working and staff weren't able to access any resources for over two weeks. I went into the school and met with the assistant headteacher to try to convince him to invest in setting their systems up correctly to end this constant fault fixing. I took a print out and showed him just how much they had spent calling me in every six months for the past two years (much more than it would have cost to set up their systems properly in the first place). Even when confronted with the school's misspending, the assistant head chose not to invest in implementing their technology correctly. Instead, we worked for three days to fix all the problems their IT manager had caused in the previous six months. By the time we left, the devices were up and running once more. Four months later, we were back at the school again.

The 'put a plaster on it' approach is one of the biggest reasons for poor productivity in UK schools. In the worst cases I have seen, schools are brought to a standstill because 'patched up' problems overwhelm their system. If a technical issue has become burdensome, then take the time to think carefully about how you will change this. Don't patch it up with a short-term solution.

3. Spend money on expertise

If you want to implement a new piece of technology, hire the right people to support you, whether this is trainers to work with your staff or technicians to install the system correctly. I have visited schools with extremely expensive equipment, whose staff don't have the foggiest idea how to use any of it. I am usually told that the cost of training was not seen as justifiable, and that senior leaders believed they could 'figure it out' themselves.

The risks of forgoing expertise are significant. First, you risk active and passive resistance to the new technology. Staff are already working above and beyond their contracts and schools are overly reliant on the passion and goodwill of their teachers. It's a big risk to risk unsettling such committed staff by dropping in technology without adequate support. If you win, you save the school a couple of thousands pound. If you lose, you risk low adoption rates, decreased productivity and lesson disruption. I know schools that are still experiencing these problems years after dropping technology into the school. They lost big time but don't even know it.

Technology is one of the best ways to improve productivity

IN 2013, THE four biggest barriers to improving school productivity were:

- Lack of capacity (not enough hours) and capability (not enough expertise)
- Geographical restrictions
- Lack of expert areas such as ICT
- Inefficient and inadequate premises

Just three years later, and cloud based platforms and collaboration tools mean that three out of those four barrier no longer exist. Let's look at how technology has impacted on each.

1. Lack of capacity and capability

Earlier in this chapter, we looked at how Broadgreen International School reduced their assessment cycle from two weeks to two days. When the project began, staff complained that they had no time to plan and improve their lesson content. Within five weeks, the assessment cycle had been reduced to two days with the use of digital assessment, and staff had hours upon hours of extra time. Technology improved their capacity.

We have also explored how smaller schools are at a disadvantage without a highly skilled school business manager on their team. With collaboration tools such as cloud platforms, schools can group together and share the expense of one, thus levelling the playing field for schools on a tight budget. Technology improving access to capability.

2. Geographical restrictions

Cloud platforms, video conferencing and collaborative documents mean that you no longer have to be in the same location to work together. At Parkroyal Community School, the leadership team no longer meet on a Tuesday night because the work is taking place continually throughout the week. Staff can work from anywhere location with an Internet connection and this has improved the speed at which the school's leaders can implement change. No more geographical restrictions.

3. Lack of expert areas such as ICT

Technology not only helps to overcome geographical restrictions, is can also give you greater access to expertise. One of the best instances of this I have seen is from the United Learning Trust academy group, with an initiative they call 'United Classroom'. The academy group has over fifty schools and a wealth of highly skilled teachers, but students have so far been consigned to the qualifications that their specific school offers. With United Classroom, this all changes as students are able to attend online lessons led by some of the best and brightest teachers in the group. With fifty plus schools to pick from, the United Learning Trust have access to an expert in pretty much every subject they will need.

With a bit of invention (working collaboratively with fellow schools) you can leverage technology to raise the capacity and capability of your school, gain access to skills and resources that were never before possible and even save money in the process. If schools are going to meet the demands of the education system then they must embrace technology as a means for improving productivity. Those that do not will simply fail.

Key Takeaways

- Focus the use of technology to improve the collaboration between teachers and departments. This can significantly speed up the improvement of your school as when information moves faster, decisions can be made quicker.
- Identify areas the technology can save money for your school and exploit them. This might be in reducing the amount of printing taking place by enabling staff to work collaboratively online, or you might want to start a cluster / group wide project and pool your collective knowledge and bargaining power when making purchases.
- Focus on implementation and training. One of the biggest drains on productivity, both in school funds and staff time, is in having technology that isn't correctly embedded into the school. That means that it either doesn't function properly, causing teachers headaches, or that teachers haven't been adequately trained and supported to use it.

CHAPTER 6

Principle Three: Improving the Consistency of Lessons

'We are what we repeatedly do. Excellence, then, is not an act but a habit"

Aristotle

Three years into her job as a maths teacher in a small secondary school, Jasmine* decided that she had had enough. The school had recently made an addition to the classroom that she found too much to bear. Every day, as she taught pythagoras and algebra to her students, she was accompanied by an unwelcome guest that stood by her side and scrutinised her every move. It was a camera mounted on a tripod, installed in order to monitor the consistency of her lessons. Its blinking red light impossible to ignore. The school had invested a grand total of £40,000 on these cameras, one for every classroom, in the hope that they would reveal standards. The unintended consequence was that it left Jasmine feeling intruded upon, exposed and criticised.

Consistency across classrooms is one of the most important measures of how well a school is performing. In 2011, The Sutton Trust identified that if you were to bring the lowest performing 10% of teachers up to the UK average, student attainment and progress would greatly improve. Jasmine's school understood that driving consistency upwards was important, but the measures they put in place were, in my view, to the detriment of its students and staff. Technology shouldn't be used to live out some Orwellian nightmare, because if teachers believe that senior leaders want to scrutinise their every move, there is a good chance they will quit. In Jasmine's case this is exactly how things played out and she is now much happier teaching in camera-free classrooms at a new school. Technology provides us plenty of new opportunities but we must be careful in how it is used to ensure we don't cross the line between supportive and invasive.

The importance of consistency on performance

IF A SCHOOL does not know how its teachers are teaching, then it can't very well know if classroom standards are good enough, or whether it is improving or not. In 2011, The Sutton Trust found that students who only have access to poor quality lessons fall as much as a whole academic year behind their peers. Perhaps this won't come as a complete surprise: of course a good teacher will get more from her students than an average one! Professor Dylan Williams has been identifying the significance of consistency on school performance for a number of years, and has found that in Canada, "variability at the classroom level is at least four times that at school level". The idea that our education system needs a large scale reform in order to improve student progress is an attractive proposition, but a growing pool of research suggests that in order to help their students, schools need to look closely at how well their teachers teach across the board. Without this attention to detail, reforming the whole system won't actually make that much difference.

Most schools I visit understand the importance of measuring consistency. The question of how to do this, however, presents senior leaders with a challenge. I believe schools are seriously behind the times because they have embraced very little technology in this area. I find that schools rely on judging consistency by measuring the output (student attainment in this case) rather than the process undertaken in the classroom. Data, without context tells you very little. You may have a student who achieves a B in their GCSEs. That looks like a good outcome, yet if we add in a second piece of information, the story changes: a year earlier, the same student was achieving A grades. So what went wrong and what could the school have done about it? The problem is that the student has already taken the exam. The opportunity to intervene has slipped by.

This is the problem when the main metric of measuring consistency is to plot test scores. Schools tend to rely on three methods to get a sense of how well their teachers are performing: observations, book trawls, and formative assessment. Only observations can really assess the rigor of a lesson and assess whether work is consistency differentiated and challenging for students. The difficulty is that observations are time intensive and can leave staff feeling like they're under scrutiny. When I speak to teachers there's often a feeling of 'us and them' when it comes to the leadership. Also, I question how much value non-subject specialists who lead lesson observations add to an experienced teacher's lesson. What value does the deputy head from English add to the veteran thirty year music teacher's lesson? Will the deputy head, who doesn't have any experience in music, be able to accurately assess how consistently challenged students are? I very much doubt it, yet this is where we are at when it comes to observations.

When students are identified as falling behind, schools typically resolve the problem by arranging an intervention. This could be in the form of catch-up sessions at lunch or after school, or working with a member of the support staff in the classroom. There are two problems with this approach. The first is that it focuses solely on student outcomes and then works backwards. If students aren't performing as well as the school would like, extra classes are arranged in an attempt to raise their attainment. There is nothing in these methods that looks first at a teacher's strengths and weaknesses in order to prevent the gap appearing in the first place. The second problem is that by the time these measures are put in place, up to a whole term may have passed. In other words, the school is playing catch up, and so are the students.

Did I say two problems? Well, to these I should add a third: after-school lessons and lunchtime revision create more work for teachers, and are only possible due to the generosity of teaching staff, who receive no extra pay for the privilege of a longer working week. These solutions extend the amount of time it takes to get the school the results it wants rather than asking how to get those results within the time it has.

The million dollar question, then: how can schools improve consistency and what is the right technology to help them in this endeavour? In this chapter, I will explain why collaboration and shared resources are the best ways for schools to improve consistency across classrooms, and how cloud software gives you the tools to achieve this more easily than was ever possible before.

Overcoming the talent myth

OUR SOCIETIES HAVE become fixated with the concept of individual talent. If we have the best and brightest on our team, then there's no doubt that we'll succeed, and the media support this narrative at every opportunity with stories of overnight success and individual brilliance winning the day.

I don't believe in natural talent. I believe that people are born with predispositions but that their aptitude is a result of the environments they exist in and the systems which support them. The 10,000 hour rule, popularised by Malcolm Gladwell in his best-selling book Outliers, delves into this concept in depth. The basic premise is that to become an expert requires 10,000 hours of purposeful practice. When we hear about prodigies, geniuses or talented individuals we rarely get the full story. Wolfgang Amadeus Mozart is the posterboy for child prodigies. He was writing symphonies by age 8 and wrote many of the world's most enduring classical pieces before his 30th birthday. Yet we don't hear that his father began teaching him to play music before he could even walk. By the time Wolfgang first performed in public at the age of six, scholars estimate that he had already accumulated thousands of hours of practice. Wolfgang didn't write his first popular piece until he was thirteen, and while that is certainly impressive we must not forget he had already had ten years of practice under his belt. We also don't hear about how Wolfgang's father, Leopold, was himself a professional musician and a strict teacher. Leopold was no slouch and he wrote A Treatise on the Fundamental Principles of Violin Playing a year before Wolfgang was born, a textbook that is still used to this day on matters of 18th century violin playing. When you deconstruct the story of Mozart you learn that it is much less about this mysterious quality we call talent and much more about purposeful practice, his environment and the systems he existed in. But what does Mozart have to do with developing consistency in classrooms?

Mozart was a product of his environment and the systems that supported his development. This is no different than the teachers in your school. Talent isn't the defining characteristic. A high performing school achieves its results because of the systems it puts in place and the environment in which teachers work. Its teachers may well be highly skilled, but the very reason that they are able to flourish is because the system supports and enables them to. This is why the very best organisations maintain such high levels of performance. They have a defined system that enables incoming staff to perform to the level that they seek. Improving consistency within a school is not a matter of getting better staff in. It is about developing a better system in which teachers will work and technology enables you to take quantum leaps in this area.

Consistency as a reflection of your systems

A SCHOOL IS an organisation where numerous individuals across different departments must coordinate and execute their actions to achieve the end goal: to give students a well rounded and meaningful education. In this type of environment it is the system (how the entire school operates) that is of most importance, even taking precedence over the staff. This is not to say that teachers are disposable. They are the most important resource within your school, but a resource is only as useful as what you can do with it. You don't turn a underperforming school around by replacing all the teachers. You create better systems and procedures for teachers to work within. This is a system led mindset versus a talent led mindset, and there is a great historical example from World War II of the difference each will bring.

In the first nine months of 1942, German U-boats had the United States Navy on the ropes and where sinking ships almost at will. "All we had to do was press the button," wrote one U-boat commander, yet on the other side of the Atlantic the story was very different. The British Navy had little troubling defending its merchant ships against the very same type of attacks that were bringing the American's to their knees. The situation didn't add up. The British command had passed on everything they knew about stopping the U-boats including tactics, sonar, and even depth-charge throwing, yet it seemed to do their new allies little good. The German U-boats continued to wreak havoc across the American coastline.

Only when you delve deeper does the important factor reveal itself. The difference in fortunes wasn't brought about due to what resources each the British and Americans had access to, but in how each Navy deployed these resources. The American Navy was led by Admiral King, a legendary naval commander and strategist. King followed what today we would call a 'tight-loose' leadership style whereby subordinates are given directions but have enough authority to interpret them how they see fit. As attacks were called in King instructed his battleships to seek out and destroy the responsible U-boats in the area, yet his captains had little success. From the beginning of 1942 up until May 1943, the US Navy sank just thirty-six U-boats, equal to one U-boat every thirteen days. Meanwhile the British Navy were coordinating their ships from a centralised command centre. Ships were given specific instructions with little room for interpretation and the U-boats quickly became the hunted as the British orchestrated their fleet to cast a net around them. The British had shared these practices with their American counterparts from the beginning, and while the American's happily took on board the technological discoveries the British had made, they ignored the organisational discoveries that were proving so successful. The American's relied on their talent over their system. Eventually the US Navy relented and the Tenth Fleet was created, a coordinated anti-submarine unit in the vision of the British centralised command centre. Within just six months of this newly established unit, the US Navy had sank seventy five U-boats, five times more than their previous strategy had produced.

The question this poses is what type of system does your school have in place? Do you have a centralised command centre like the British did or have you slid into a 'tight-loose' management structure that failed the Americans?

Systems over resources

THE TRUE VALUE of the British approach wasn't in dealing out strict orders. It was the collaboration of many individuals to advance a single goal through improved knowledge and insight.

I believe that one of the keys to improving the consistency across your school is to bolster the collective knowledge of teachers, and technology plays a big role in this. By working collectively, it is easy for teachers to create bespoke learning resources that draw on the strengths of the individuals involved. For example a science department can decide as a team which teacher is responsible for creating Year 9 resources on photosynthesis, and who will create Year 9 resources on the periodic table. Rather than everyone creating their own individual resources for every topic and rushing to get it all done on time, the department divides up the work, and shares what it creates. Cloud platforms easily empower you to do this. The department can create a shared folder that all members of the team can access. Teachers can upload their existing resources or create new ones. From there they can comment on one another's work, edit or suggest revisions, all without the need to print off any paper, arrange any meetings or even be in the same room together. Removing these barriers enables staff to work more closely to pool their collective knowledge. This drives quality higher.

This is a concept inspired by the Finnish model of teaching, wherein teachers spend hours together each week creating resources in precisely this collaborative style. If it wasn't already clear by now, I'm a great admirer of the Finnish education system because of its progressive practices, which go against the assumptions that slow up the UK's system. Finnish teachers have the freedom to work together in this way because they only teach four lessons a day (and yet Finland consistently outperforms most other developed countries in terms of literacy and numeracy). Whilst teachers in the UK are unlikely to ever have the luxury of a four-lesson schedule, they can still enjoy the benefits of collaborating by using cloud technology like G Suite to work on documents together without having to be in the same room.

It's a simple concept, but different to how most schools currently work, and potentially revolutionary. There are many benefits, but the most important one is that it makes it clear from the outset what the expected quality of learning resources and identifies teachers needing additional support or training. Remember, if schools could bring the lowest performing 10% of teachers up to the UK average, then they would greatly boost attainment and student progress.

It is substantially more useful to be able to proactively identify which of your teachers may need additional support going into a new term than reactively trying to catch students up after a term because classroom consistency varied too greatly.

I helped implement this kind of system with Parkroyal and Invicta primary schools as part of their development and they are already enjoying the benefits. Each school have over 30,000 approved shared documents that can be accessed by teachers and senior leaders at any time. Teachers at Invicta comment that they spend less time planning lessons from scratch and more time improving their existing ones. Senior leaders are confident that they know the content and quality of their school's lessons. Introducing collaborative working with G Suite was one of the key factors that enabled teachers at Invicta to save 87 minutes from their weekly schedule and senior leaders, 4 hours, both while performing to a higher standard.

Collaboration was also one of the key reasons why Broadgreen International School was able to improve maths GCSE results by 25% when I worked with their staff in 2014. The aim of our project was to use technology to raise student progress. The first stage, which involved digitising assessment, is discussed in the Improving Capability chapter. The second stage of the project required teachers to share best practice and collaborate on teaching resources. This proved most beneficial to classroom differentiation, which had been identified as a challenge for the department by leadership. Reducing the assessment cycle from two weeks to two days enabled teachers to free up time so that they could share best practice more often with each other. Interestingly, regardless of their years in school, I found that teachers relied predominantly on what they had been taught at the start of their career. Between just eight staff there were four generations of teacher, each who had gone through a different variation of initial teacher training. As staff pooled their knowledge, even the most experienced staff (15 years +) learnt new strategies from the younger teachers (3 years in) who had learnt the latest child development strategies through their initial training.

Enabling teachers at Broadgreen to collaborate often culminated not only in better learning materials and lesson planning, but also in a significantly upgraded

GCSE exam revision pack that included video explainers and digital resources for students. The development of a 'centralised command centre' in the maths department had a significant impact. The cumulative effect of the project's aims, teachers' efforts and a lot of hard work was reflected in the GCSE performance. Independent work improved by 97%, group work improved by 80% and the department achieved a 25% improvement on its year on year GCSE performance. True testament to the power of collaboration.

Ending 'Just in Time' Lesson Planning

CONTRAST THE EXPERIENCES of the schools I've just talked about to the following real life example:

It was the middle of the school day, and Janet*, Deputy Head of Farm Hill Primary*, was sitting at her desk in a state of alarm. Janet was a proud deputy, and confident that her school offered its students a fine education. Yet she'd just caught sight of something that made her begin to questioning that. What was the offending item? Nothing more than the outline of a leaf.

The leaf was a Year 6 Science worksheet. The accompanying lesson plan was simple: the children were required to colour the leaf in, with the aim of learning its parts. Herein lay the reason for Janet's shock: it was nothing more than the outline of a leaf. This for Year

6 children who, the following academic year, would be expected to master the intricacies of photosynthesis, learn the periodic table and understand the structure of an atom. The teacher responsible had quite happily confirmed that he had been using this sheet for years. It was something he had found online and, as it turned out, he had several more lesson plans that were pretty similar. This was news to Janet. In truth, the senior leadership team had little idea of the specific content any of the teachers used in the classroom, and had always trusted in their experience and expertise. Her immediate reaction was one of anger, followed by the realisation that something had to change in order to make sure such lessons were a thing of the past.

When you leave consistency to chance, this is the kind of situation you can easily find yourself in as a school leader. I have retold Janet's story, not to humiliate or cast judgement upon teachers whose lesson plans are of questionable quality, but in order to understand why these situations arise and to demonstrate how they can be avoided. As I see it, there are three reasons why poor lesson planning happens. The first is that teachers do not have enough time in their working week for lesson planning. The result of this is that when time-saving options (like downloadable resources) present themselves, teachers are likely to take them. It is human nature to take the path of least resistance, and once you cross the line into the world of online resources, where is your incentive to go back?

The Internet is full of education sites where teachers upload and exchange lesson plans. You can learn a lot from just viewing the interactions taking place online.

Teacher A: *Help! I have a Year 5 Science class tomorrow and need a worksheet that teaches electricity. Any suggestions?*
Teacher B: *Yep, I used this one recently and it seemed to hit the mark. Let me send you the link.*
Teacher C: *Here's one I always use - kids always enjoy it.*

I've termed this phenomenon 'just in time' lesson planning. Join any number of Facebook teacher groups and you'll see exchanges like the one above taking place on a near daily basis. The worksheet that Teacher A ends up with might be fantastic; it might also be average, or worse. Internet resources are not vetted and there is little to stop teachers ending up with glorified colouring sheets.

The second reason for poor lesson plans is that senior leaders do not have easy access to teaching resources. So, when a subpar worksheet gets added to a teacher's portfolio, it might be years before it is identified as below standard. The third reason is the teacher's own pedagogical knowledge. This is a significant issue for UK schools when you consider how little training and professional development teachers are offered compared to their peers abroad. In Canada, for example, schools spend 10% of their budget on training and development.

In England, that number is just 0.5%. Historically, there is little research that looks at the importance of pedagogical knowledge on a teacher's performance. However, of the work that has been undertaken there is a growing evidence base that a teacher's pedagogical knowledge is linked to higher student achievement. Studies by Hill, Rowan and Ball (2005), Baumert et al. (2010), and Voss, Kunter and Baumert (2011) all support this. Reports by The Sutton Trust, the UK's most respected education think-tank, as well as reports from the OECD, frequently rate a teacher's pedagogical knowledge as the most critical factor to the quality of learning. It should not be surprising that the UK currently sits nineteen places below Canada on the PISA world education rankings for reading, and seventeen places below for maths. However, rather than looking at these statistics as depressing confirmation of the struggles of the UK education system, we must ask ourselves what schools can do in the face of these odds and how they can bridge this gap.

Cloud technology is within any schools reach and its collaboration features address all three of these problems. Collaboration aids pedagogical development because it allows teachers to see how their peers work and to learn from them. Collaboration saves teachers time because they do not each have to create an entire year's worth of resources, instead sharing the workload. Through software like G Suite, resources are also visible to senior leaders, who can then decide if they meet the expected standards. If not they can proactively address inconsistencies before they manifest in the classroom.

It was with this collaborative spirit that Dame Sally Coates improved teaching and learning at Burlington Danes Academy. When she arrived at the school in 2008, it was falling (rated as Requiring Improvement). One of her greatest concerns was the lack of academic rigour in lessons. She understood that you can't manage consistency when you leave it to chance. To resolve this, she stipulated that teachers must hand in their lesson plans each Friday for the week ahead. Dame Sally and her senior leaders would sign off on each lesson plan, and when they came across ones that didn't meet the expectations the teacher would be told and offered support to improve upon it. Her system worked, and Dame Coates was able to take the school from requiring improvement to outstanding in five years. She recognised that to improve learning for students, she needed to address consistency if she was to develop the level of excellence she imagined. That she did this without technology in a pre-cloud era is all the more impressive. Today, with platforms such as G Suite schools can implement the same quality control methods that Dame Sally put into practice effortlessly. Her example shows the impact that managing consistency of lessons can have on a school, and coupled with the collaborative power of cloud technology, many of the biggest challenges we see in our schools can be solved in a very straightforward way.

Key Takeaways

- You can't control quality until you first control consistency. By using technology to improve collaboration and communication, you improve the transparency throughout the school, and teachers will work to a consistently higher level.

- Systems matter more than resources. It's not a question of what you have at your disposal (teachers / devices / content), but what you do with those resources that improves learning outcomes. One of technology's biggest strengths is it's ability to better organise a school. Take advantage of this potential and you'll be able to control consistency to a much greater degree.

- You job as a school leader is to create a consistent environment for your teachers. This means that everyone should be able to work in a consistent way, whether they're at home or at school. Classrooms should be consistent, with little variation in technology, and most of all, teachers should receive a consistent message of what is expected of them.

PART 3

[REBOOTING YOUR SCHOOL]

CHAPTER 7

Environment Dictates Technology

The first rule of any technology used in an organisation is that automation applied to an efficient operation will magnify the efficiency. The second is that automation applied to an inefficient operation will magnify the inefficiency.
Bill Gates

Waterford Primary Academy* sits on a quiet and leafy street of a well-to-do northern suburb, famous for its champagne bars and footballers' wives.

For several years now, it has enjoyed a reputation as a leader in technology in the local authority. While other schools were dithering over whether or not to 'go digital' in the early noughties, Waterford were already thinking about how to equip their classrooms for the future. It made the local papers in 2011 when it became one of the first schools in the UK to use iPads in lessons, and has often received high praise for its eagerness to adopt new technology. Every year, parents raise funds towards improving engagement with technology, and often collect upwards of £30,000. Former Chancellor of the Exchequer George Osborne, Google Education and Apple Education have all visited its premises to admire the gamut of devices in play.

I was invited by Waterford in 2016 to carry out a review of how effectively it was using technology. When I conducted an anonymous survey of teachers, ninety-three percent felt that technology had not helped teaching and learning. When asked why, they said that it was unreliable and that they had never been trained to use it. Staff had twenty-six different variations of technology to grapple with. How much training did Waterford offer its teachers to manage such a complex set of systems? Less than eight hours per year.

I could talk at length about Waterford Primary. It's a school I've known since 2012. They first invited me in to find a solution to the problems they were experiencing after only a year with iPads. In late 2016, I was invited in once more to help them cope with the difficulties the iPads presented them with. After spending half a day evaluating how they were using technology, it was clear that its classrooms were overflowing with gadgets they didn't know how to use. This included (brace yourself): 60 Windows laptops running XP, 30 Windows desktops running VISTA, 30 iPads running iOS 9, 30 iPads running iOS 7, 30 iPads running iOS 5, Lego Mindstorm coding hardware, Sphero coding hardware, SIMs for managing student data, Target Tracker for managing student assessment, a school server, an iCloud shared drive, a Dropbox shared drive, a parent communication system, a VLE (virtual learning environment), a school internal messaging system, a school Twitter profile, and 3 different brands of interactive whiteboards running 10 different variations of software. The school worked with three different ICT support companies who, unsurprisingly, did not work together very well and tended to blame one another for the school's spiralling ICT issues. On ICT support alone, the school was spending over £30,000 a year, yet they had little to show for it.

The headteacher was under no illusion that the school was full of tech; the problem was she was proud of it. In fact, she was keen to buy even more technology, believing that newer software might solve their mounting ICT woes. The school's reputation as a 'technology leader' made it difficult for them to think critically about how they were implementing technology; instead the motto seemed to have become 'tech for tech's sake'.

I have already spoken about the serious problems created by buying technology for the sake of it. It lacks impact and wastes both time and money. In this chapter, I want to explore these problems in the context of how you develop the environment of your school. We're delving into the discipline of the architecture of technology, and how you go about designing exactly how your school operates at a person to person level. This is a complex field, so I'm only going to focus on one element of it: that you are able to design the work environment for the teachers and staff in your school through the technology you select. This is something that most organisations, not just schools, don't even realise is possible.

As a leader, one of your most vital contributions should be deciding upon a vision and leading your school to achieve the goals that are part of it. Before committing to any device or software, you must therefore ask, 'Does this technology support the environment I want to create? How does this fit into our vision?' If you don't do this, your school will never become an optimum environment for learning. The technology, like it did at Waterford, will end up controlling and limiting the working environment. What should be happening is that your working environment should determine the technology you bring in.

The problems that stem from a basic lack of forward planning are endless. Waterford is a prime example. Their teachers don't get adequately trained, so a teacher confident with technology in one classroom may not be able to easily move rooms as there's a different set of technology to use. Due to the lack of any centralised and supporting system, computers, whiteboards and iPads can't be synced up, meaning that work can't be passed from one device to another. The school has over thirty different variations of software to fulfil just a handful of activities, yet none of it communicates with one another. This means that the work on one device (iPad) can't be accessed from another (Windows laptop). The school has a vision to become one of the country's leading technology-led primary schools, but this will never happen with their current mindset because ironically it is technology that is holding them back.

Compare the list of software and gadgets at Waterford to that of a business with a similar number of staff. In a business you will find:

- Company computers
- Company phone
- Company business system
- Boardroom presentation system

The company will have a contract for the same model of phone, use the same brand of computers and have a single company-wide business system. When an upgrade is needed, all devices are upgraded at once. This means that all employees work in a unified way.

Sounds straightforward? This is how it should be, for schools as well as businesses.

Which technology you choose for your school depends entirely on the environment you want to create. Technology is a wonderful thing and it allows us to work in new ways, but it is not limitless. When you commit to a certain piece of technology, you commit to work in the way in which it has been designed. Take iPads for example. Apple designed them as a one user device, and that created some headaches for schools using them as shared devices with students. Until 2015, there was no functionality to have user profiles on an iPad and they didn't easily integrate into the Windows servers that schools relied on. Despite all the brilliant new opportunities the technology offered, it came with a major limitation: it was difficult to move work off the device which vastly reduced its impact in the classroom. Chromebooks are the latest in-vogue technology in education. They're portable, lightweight and very low cost laptops, and schools are buying them up rapidly. Their limitation? You do all your work in the cloud through Google Suite for Education, and this means you'd better have a good wireless network installed. Pros and cons. All technology brings both.

I want to introduce you to a concept I've developed called 'building from the outside in'. Understanding this concept will enable you to take full advantage of the benefits that technology, brings while mitigating any downsides.

Environment before devices

WHEN YOU COME to develop the technology throughout your school, you must realise that it doesn't exist in isolation and will have a significant impact on your staff. To match the needs of your organisation and staff, you must assess technology across four levels.

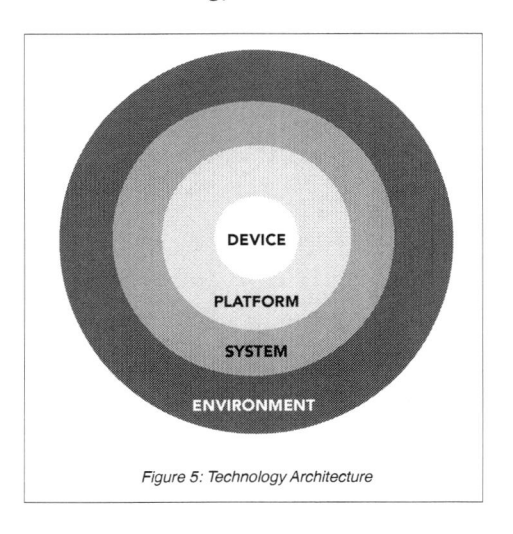

Figure 5: Technology Architecture

The Device: this is the physical product such as a desktop computer, laptop or iPad.

The Platform: this is the operating software of the device. Apple iPads run on iOS whereas Microsoft laptops use Windows, for example.

The System: this is one or many systems in which staff carry out their jobs. In a school you have an assessment system, for example.

The Environment: this is the human element of how an organisation functions. Do you want people to work in a collaborative way? Do you want people to be able to access content whenever they need it?

Think of the technology architecture of building an organisation like the architecture involved in building a house. When you build a house you work with an architect to develop concept sketches of your vision. When you think about your dream house, you think of it in terms of the **environment** it will create for you. Will it have a grand room? A large kitchen that is great for cooking? Will the rooms be filled with natural light? Once you're happy, you commission the build and hire contractors, engineers and builders. These are the **systems** that will turn those plans into a reality. But houses aren't built with barehands, and your builders will need the right tools. Diggers, cranes, trucks, hammers, nails and much much more. These physical tools are named **platforms** in the technology world. After months of hard work your house is finally built, but hang on a minute. There's no furniture in it. What will you sit on? What will you cook on? How will you wash? So you take a trip to IKEA and stock up. This final act is all about picking the right **devices**.

We all know the steps involved in building a house. You wouldn't go out and buy thousands of pounds of new furniture before having your first meeting with the architect. Neither would you become so attached to your long serving corner sofa that you attempt to design your new house around it.

However, when it comes to technology architecture, the process isn't as easy to visualise. The common mistake in many organisations, not just schools, is that the organisation is developed from the inside out. Devices are chosen and the organisation is developed around them.

This approach creates a serious ripple effect. At the platform level, you begin to see compatibility issues: at the system level, you experience a lack of integration; and at the environment level, you see a lack of productivity and efficiency.

At the device level, Apple products don't talk to Microsoft products that well, just as Smart's interactive whiteboard software is not the same as Promethean's. Your assessment systems may work on Microsoft platforms, but they don't integrate with Android tablets. You originally equipped teachers with mobile devices to improve their productivity, but now you find they can't move work from their laptop to other school devices, and the assessment system doesn't integrate with either: is any of this sounding familiar?

Problems at the systems level

THIS PROBLEM WOULDN'T be so bad if we were just dealing with one issue at each level. That way we could just remove the offending piece of the technological puzzle, replacing it with a compatible, integrated alternative. Unfortunately, it's not so simple. Schools have multiple variations of technology at the device, platform and system levels. It is the system level in particular that is most problematic within schools.

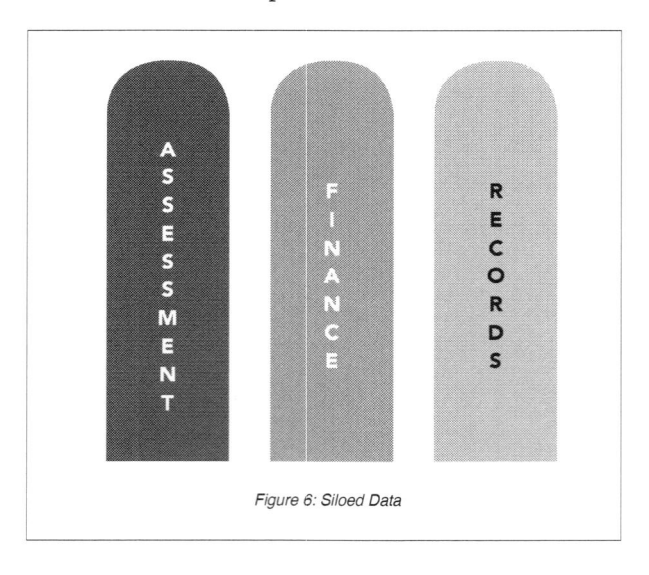

Figure 6: Siloed Data

Every school needs to capture and manage key data. This falls into three categories: assessment, finance and student / staff records. Typically, a school will have a dedicated system to manage each, but this is where problems begin. These systems rarely integrate with one another and are siloed off. This puts huge pressure on staff.

Take the following example. Imagine that you have a group of twenty students who are predicted to achieve

Ds or below in their upcoming GCSEs. Last year, you had a similar scenario and you arranged subject catch up sessions twice per week and extra classroom support with a teaching assistant. Fifteen of the twenty students went on to achieve a C grade, but this year, budgets are tighter. You can't afford to run both additional catch up sessions and rota in support staff, so which do you choose? You should be able to login to your school's systems and answer this within 60 seconds, yet this is rarely the case. What I've found is that the systems that schools rely on can't map the learning return on investment (ROI) from the initiatives that are put in place. Rather, school leaders rely on their intuition or are lucky enough to have a maths whizz who is unlucky enough to be tasked with pouring over all the data. Manual data analysis takes hours upon hours and personal intuition is a poor substitute for definitive data.

The world outside of education is undergoing what is known as the 'big data' revolution. Big data is defined as extremely large data sets that are analysed computationally to reveal patterns, trends, and associations, especially relating to human behaviour and interactions. It's how Facebook targets you with relevant adverts based on what you like and comment on, how Uber know the exact time it needs more taxis on the road, and how supermarkets know exactly which products should be placed on which shelves. It enables organisations to predict an outcome with a unnerving level of accuracy. Facebook is so good at this that after you have liked 300 posts, it's better able to predict your behaviour than your own spouse!

The implications for big data technology in education are huge. You would know exactly which students were going to fall behind before any test was taken. So, how do you make sure that those twenty students achieve higher than predicted grades on a restricted budget? Two ways. The first is that there must be no more siloed information. Schools must operate on a system that fully integrates data across assessment, finance and student / staff records into one centralised place. No more siloed data.

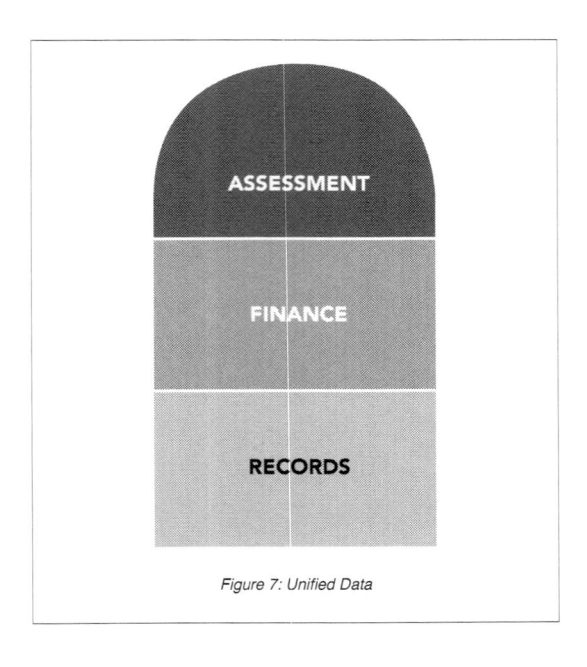

Figure 7: Unified Data

Second, schools must rely on technology to analyse and predict trends. Facebook doesn't employ people to cross reference what you're liking and commenting on. They employ technology to do that. The people they employ decide what to do with the findings of that data. This is no different from schools. If you're manually cross referencing data, printing off reams of spreadsheets or creating 'war-boards', then you're doing something wrong. You're spending time analysing data when you could be acting on it.

The technology I'm talking about is no longer some pipe dream. You don't need the deep pockets of Facebook to take advantage of it either. The new wave of school data systems is already bringing big data technology into schools across the UK, giving you access to a single centralised system that analyses the data so that you can spend more time acting on it.

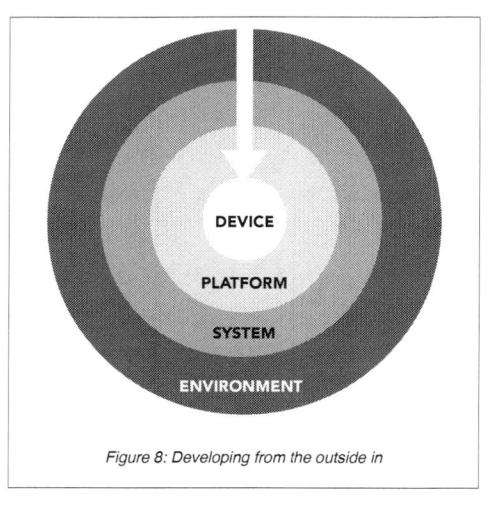

Figure 8: Developing from the outside in

Developing from the outside in.

THE KEY TO developing your school when it comes to technology is to develop from the outside in.

Start with the environment you want to create for staff to work in. Do you want them to work long hours? Should working together be easy or difficult? How will they access files and documents? Once you have a vision of what an average day looks like for a teacher, you can begin looking for the right systems to turn it into reality. With your systems chosen you then know what platforms are supported. Do your systems integrate with Apple, Google, Microsoft, Promethian and Smart? These are the main platforms that dominate education, and you will need to know which are supported and which are not. Finally, you begin selecting the devices that will be used by students and staff. This might mean that you can't adopt the device that is currently popular, but ultimately this won't matter. With a strong technology architecture in place, you'll be able to achieve far more than by blindly buying up education technology that is currently popular. By following the rules, you'll end up with technology that is compatible, integrated and effective. Best of all, this 'outside-in' approach will mean it is the culture of your school and its teaching and learning objectives that drive development.

Only a few years ago, having any real technological control over your school's working environment was out of the picture. The cost of these technologies was astronomically expensive, and the expertise required to maintain it, beyond all but the most technologically gifted. The advances in cloud platforms big data systems have changed all of this. Today, any school can reap the rewards of such technology.

Less is More

THE BIGGEST PROBLEM facing schools across the UK right now is not that they don't have enough access to technology. It is that they actually have too much. From research carried out by OECD, only a handful of countries are ahead of the UK, in terms of how much access children have to computers.

If we keep in mind the complexities of technology architecture, and how little is spent on staff development within UK education (0.5%), it is easy to see why technology is ineffective and complex in our schools. Implementation is much more than setting technology up into school. It is about how effectively it integrates into a typical teacher's day and whether it improves or worsens it.

This should act as a wake up call for those who believe the problem lies in a lack of computing resources. The reason why we see almost no educational benefit from technology in our education system is because there's little implementation.

To begin making technology more effective in school, you will first need to begin phasing a lot of it out. This is an unsettling thought for schools who have scrimped and saved for years to be able to afford the latest technology for the classroom. However, you can't hope to improve your school if technology isn't supporting it. Technology, despite its vast potential, has become a key element in destabilising classroom consistency simply because of its complexity. Things start to go wrong quickly when technology doesn't work well. Staff begin to take shortcuts or workarounds are found, because there are no other options.

Nothing epitomises this better than the explosion of iPads into schools. Until 2016, iPads were built to be a one user device, with little compatibility to be able to share work anywhere other than through Apple's own iCloud storage platform. Schools began buying up iPads by the trolley full and deploying them as shared resources. This is where the first problem occurred. Schools were dismayed to find that iPads weren't compatible out of the box with their Microsoft servers, and students couldn't move work on or off their device like they would on a laptop or desktop. Instantly, this reduced what an iPad could be used for in the classroom because there was no way for students to save work to their home folder. Hardware workarounds were eventually found, but schools had to spend more money on installation and setup. It eased compatibility problems for iPads, but often the solution didn't always work that well. That is the definition of a workaround, afterall.

Next, schools found that many of the most established assessment and student data systems didn't integrate with iPads. This meant that staff would have to run both a Windows laptop and an iPad. Not a huge concern in itself, but problematic when you consider that teachers now needed to be comfortable with two different operating systems instead of one.

It might look like iPads were the wrong decision for many schools and that they fall into the category of technology that isn't simple or effective, but that isn't the case. iPads and the growth of mobile devices in education have highlighted how schools are myopically focused on buying devices without considering the larger impact across the school. The iPad is a disruptive technology and it challenged the perception of the PC / laptop as the dominating device. Like all disruptive technology, it highlighted inadequacies in the systems we have built. The iPad is the most revolutionary device in education since the advent of the printed book. The lesson to learn is that we must never get attached to the systems that we build in education, otherwise we become a slave to them.

It won't make a huge difference whether you use Chromebooks, Microsoft laptops or iPads in the classroom this year. It is the systems that are already embedded in your school that should come under review. The level of personalisation of learning that schools are able to achieve with mobile devices is simply unmatched, and they are a central piece in the development of the future of education. The problem is that mobile devices are designed to work with the cloud, and school systems are not cloud ready. This presents you with one important question to answer. Do you want to explore new opportunities and take advantage of the full potential that technology offers for education or do you want to experience the pain and struggle as you try to hang on to the past?w

CHAPTER 8

The Time to Act is Now

"You don't have to be great to start, but you have to start to be great"

Zig Ziglar

The effects of technology, an ageing population and true globalisation are producing unrivalled change in the world today. I believe that we are on the cusp of a new age and it will redefine how our governments act and how our public institutions are run. Technology has been with us for a long time, but it is only just starting to significantly disrupt our everyday lives. Before long a Jetson-like world filled with driverless cars, artificial intelligence and robot workers will be a reality. The benefits will be huge but then industries will be disrupted, entire professions will disappear and governments will take time to react. If you don't believe this is the case, then you only need to look at history for clues. When it comes to revolutions, we tend to think of them as a single defining event, but the reality is quite different.

We might imagine that one day hunter gathers woke up, downed their spears and picked up scythes to begin the Agricultural Revolution, but the reality is it took over 2000 years to happen across just the Fertile Crescent alone. It took up to 200 years in some areas just to domesticate wheat, a grain that now makes up a large portion of the Western diet.

The Industrial Revolution began when the first textile factory to use a spinning frame opened in 1743, but it wasn't until the mid 19th Century, over 100 years later that we really saw a significant impact in our country as people flocked to the cities and England became a global trading power.

There are lots of names for the time we're living in. The Information Age, the Third Industrial Revolution, The Anthropocene epoch; personally, I think they all fall short. What we're really in is the Technological Age, and we have been since the middle of the 20th Century. The big changes we're experiencing are due to the maturity of technology that has been a long time coming. As the world becomes more connected, the rate of change increases, and the dominating technology of the revolution matures in half the time it previously did. It took 200 years to mature wheat in the Agricultural Revolution. It took 100 years to mature the steam engine in the Industrial Revolution. Now it has taken 50 years to mature the computer, the defining technology of the Technological Revolution.

Education has been under pressure due to student numbers, government cuts and recruitment shortages for a long time. In the coming years, these will escalate into what will be nothing short of a earthquake. By 2023, there will be an additional one million children in UK schools, by 2020 the government has announced it will make £3 billion of cuts to education and today we are already in the grips of a serious teacher recruitment and retention problem.

Knowing this earthquake is coming allows you to prepare for it. Fail to prepare and you'll experience the full brunt and devastation of it first hand.

Preparing for the earthquake

THERE ARE ONLY three ways to overcome problems on this scale, and schools have already exhausted two.

Since 2008, the average teacher now works 10% more hours per week according to the data from the Annual Teachers Workload Survey. The trigger for this was the increase in accountability measures introduced by the Government at the time, and schools relied on teachers working longer hours to meet the new demands. Today, teachers work close to sixty hours per week; in other words there are no hours left in the day. Teachers are maxed out.

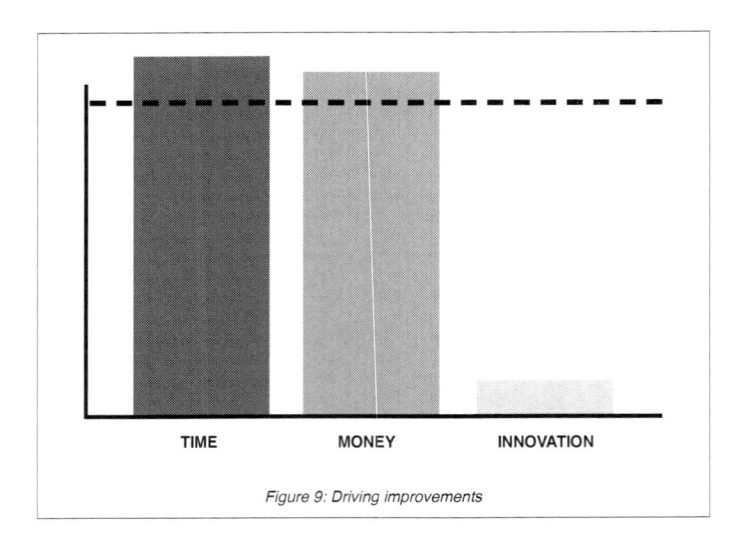

Figure 9: Driving improvements

When teachers have no more capacity to work extra hours, schools begin spending money to hire more staff. In 2007, there were 163,800 teaching assistants. By 2015, this had more than doubled to 387,600. If the education system can support these numbers, then this is no problem, but as a ratio of school spending, wages significantly accelerated. Today staffing costs take up around 80% of a school's budget putting them in a precarious position. With increases in school funding highly unlikely, schools are running out of money.

Throughout this same period, there was little talk about how innovation, specifically through the use of new technology, could ease these problems. You might be surprised to learn that G Suite for Education, one of the cloud platform technologies capable of transforming schools everywhere, launched all the way back in 2006.

The option to innovate has always been there. The problem is that, in the past schools have relied on spending more time and money to fix their problems. However, this must change, and it must change today.

To begin innovating, you need only remember three key points.

1. *You must commit*

The right time to begin is now. I've worked with hundreds of schools in the past few years, and I've learnt one key lesson: commitment is everything. Invicta Primary School was one of the most successful projects I've been involved in. From beginning to end it took just over a week to get the green light for that project. That is lightning fast by education standards. With other schools, I've entertained meetings and answered questions for months before senior leaders decided whether to commence with a project. They tell me that all of these meetings and the months of delayed decisions arise because of the need for careful planning and consideration, but in truth, it is down to a lack of commitment. It's easy to bring in more decision makers, often governors, to share the burden of commitment but the schools where our work has had the most impact are the ones where we've never met governors. Instead, the leadership team makes the decision, which they then take to their governors. The team here at LearnMaker can throw everything we've got into the project, but what we can't do is become the headteacher of the school. We can't inspire people to follow us the way a headteacher can. We can't deliver the morning briefings to spread the message. We can't become the personification of the future of the school. School leadership teams get worried about undertaking projects in busy periods of the school year. I can't think of a better time personally to implement technology that's biggest strength is in saving time and improving collaboration.

2. Don't be lead astray

Education, more so than other industries, is filled with followers. The majority of schools I've met buy their technology based on what other schools are using. When I meet that other school, they tell me the same, that they bought their technology because they saw someone else using it. If you follow the chain backwards, you eventually find the source; clever marketing; or a presence at a large trade show; or a supplier agreement with the local authority or government. For well over a decade, schools have been led by the nose into spending over £1 billion on technology by the companies that sell it. The problem is not that companies are doing this, it's that schools are following others blindly. Better decisions come from better questions, and the first question you need to ask when looking at technology is, "What impact is it delivering?" Right now the first question schools ask is, "What is everyone else using?

3. Embrace change and think ahead

The schools that experience the most pain from imposed changes are those that are inert. I saw this particularly when coding was introduced onto the primary computing curriculum in 2014. Despite digital skills having the largest skills gap in the UK, coding's introduction provoked outrage within some areas of the education system. While scores of people complained and protested this change, other schools got their heads down and embraced the challenge as well as the opportunity it brought. At LearnMaker, we ran coding projects with primary schools to build and release a fully working iPad app in just five days. The schools we worked with excelled, and after the project they found themselves speaking about their excellence at national education conferences. Meanwhile, those who were inert were still complaining and contesting the changes foisted upon them. What did their protests achieve? Nothing. The curriculum wasn't revised and coding is still part of it. All that happened was that they lost hours of their own time and placed themselves in a negative mindset, not an ideal place from which to inspire learning.

The benefits of innovating with technology

HERE ARE SOME of the tangible things to expect when you innovate through technology:

Better outcomes - the better staff can perform, the better student outcomes are. Teachers go into education to benefit their students, so what could be more rewarding than seeing them do better?

Less stress – when you're passionate about what you do and you work in a supported environment, doing your job becomes less stressful and more rewarding.

More time for what's important – Cloud platforms can save the average classroom teacher fifty-six hours per year. The leadership team at Invicta saved four hours per week. That's over 138 extra hours per year each! Spend it enjoying some well earned downtime with your feet up eating pizza or reinvest it into what's important to you. Either way, you'll spend less time on paperwork and more on what you're passionate about (even if that is eating pizza).

Recognition – When you excel in a field, others want to know why. Don't be surprised if you're asked to speak at conferences, give talks or have a queue of local schools wanting to visit. These are all things that have happened with schools I've worked with and they all advance your career.

The ability to attract great teachers – when you're a beacon of excellence, you attract others who share those values. High performing schools have less trouble recruiting high performing teachers than their lower performing peers. Having an innovative, technology-supported environment is another way to differentiate yourself from other schools in your area and attract the best staff.

Retaining your best staff - The first key to developing a great team is to ensure you don't lose your best people. The loss of a few key personnel can have a huge impact on both performance and cost. At one school I worked with, the headteacher's PA said at the end of the project that she could never go back to working in a school that didn't use a cloud platform. That's strong retention right there.

Myths you must overcome

IF YOU'VE READ this far, then there's a good chance that you're committed to using technology to better your school. To ensure that you get the process right, you must avoid falling for the three myths that lead schools astray:

Myth 1: I will get the same results if I do it myself

This is the misconception that hurts schools the most. The reality is that there is no comparison between an expert and an amateur. To reach the level of an expert, you have to put in 10,000 hours of purposeful practice. You might have dabbled in technology and read as much as you can find on the Internet, but this is ill preparation once you take charge of a large scale technology project.

An expert will achieve high results in a short space of time. An amateur on the other hand, will achieve only mediocre results even over a long time.

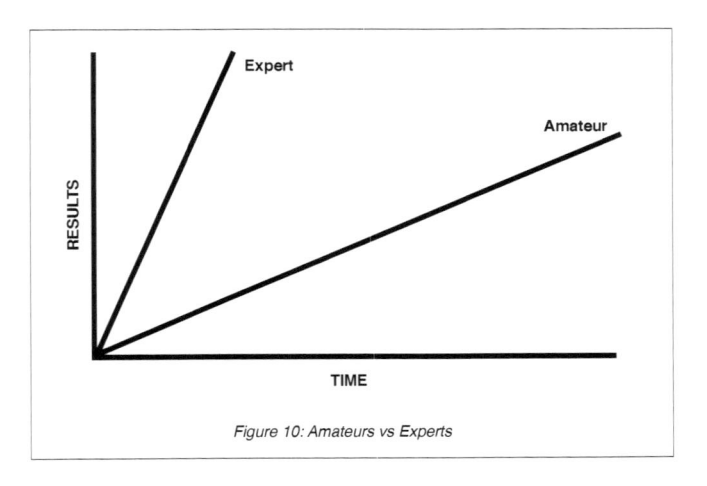

Figure 10: Amateurs vs Experts

Ensure the success of your project by engaging an expert. Moving your entire school to the cloud, for example, is not a simple or straightforward process, and there are a multitude of factors that will need to be taken into account to ensure it is a success. Without the right implementation you will not see the results that you expect from the technology

I want to expand on just how important implementation is when it comes to technology in the next myth.

Myth 2: An expert is more costly

A lot of us have trouble with the concept of lifetime costs and we make a lot of our buying decisions based on the upfront cost alone. If you pay an expert £10,000 to deliver a project, then you might say that it is more expensive than if you did it myself. That isn't true however, because you're assuming that you will achieve the same outcome as the expert. You won't. You're not paying £10,000 for the expert's time. You're paying £10,000 for the result they will provide you.

When people take on something of this scale themselves, it is very easy to make a lot of mistakes, and mistakes cause problems. Eventually, an amateur has to make a decision; to pay an expert to come in to rectify the mistakes made **and** deliver the project, or to simply abandon the project and with it, all the time and money that has already been invested.

Myth 3: Technology automatically creates value

Technology has no inherent value other than what you can get from it. It's easy to get lulled in by the excitement of technology, assuming that things such as student engagement will lead to better outcomes. Sure, if you walk into a Year 10 maths lesson with thirty iPads then you've instantly got the attention of the students more so than if you had walked in with thirty textbooks. Yet the resource doesn't matter that much, it's what you do with it that counts. If I couldn't read then a textbook would be pretty redundant in helping me to learn maths, as it would be if I were given an iPad with no structured learning objective to use it for. Technology only begins to have an impact when it is implemented correctly throughout the school and embedded into the curriculum.

There are considerable risks to going it alone and trying to do it all yourself. Technology is complex, and undertaking any large project requires deep expertise. You may say that there's no money in the budget to bring in expertise. If that's the case there's an easy solution for your project. Cancel it and launch it once you *do* have the budget. Otherwise, you risk wasting what little you have undertaking a project that is unlikely to achieve the results that you expect.

I meet a lot of schools who say they use Google Suite, and this is true. For example, these schools predominately use just the free online storage part. However, they still run an onsite server for their main file storage, office documents are still completed in Microsoft, and collaboration only happens in person around a table. There's no real benefit from selecting tools from Google Suite. What we've explored over the course of this book is that the tools that technology provides are largely irrelevant. It is the new ways in which to work that are most important. In the case of using Google Suite for Education, the benefits for you and your school only materialise when you embrace the Google way of working.

The difference between the best and the rest

THE BIGGEST DIFFERENCE that I've noticed over the years that separates the very best schools from the rest is how humble they are. These school leaders have created amazing schools, full of vibrant learning and passionate teachers. Often they're already using technology more effectively than other schools, yet when I meet them the first thing they want to know is how to do even more.

The ability to listen is key. I've worked with one school in particular for over four years and in that time they've gone backwards. The reason why is that they just don't take advice onboard. When they seek out my help, what they really want is for me to validate their plan. I never can. The technology in this school is a mess, despite the tens of thousands they pump into it every year. They're solely focused on buying more devices and gadgets at the expense of developing any environment in which they all work together. The last time I visited they were showing off new programmable robots for computing. They've never been used in the four months they've owned them because they didn't put any money aside for training. No-one knows how they work and over £20,000 was spent on them. Every year, the staff survey reveals that teachers are more stressed and less confident about using technology in their classrooms, and each year the school go out and buy more to throw into the mix. They're completely blinkered in their thinking.

If you're going to engage with experts, then listen to them. They've spent thousands of hours honing their craft, experienced hundreds of different scenarios and will already know the solutions for your needs. The value they will bring to you is far more than their fee. You simply can't do it alone.

Where to next?

THERE IS NOTHING in this book that isn't achievable in your school. You may feel that you're stuck in a rut in your own school or the pressures from above are just too much to bear. Getting through each day might be your biggest focus right now. This is inertia, and unless you want to spend the rest of your career working this way, then you must look for a way out. No-one is coming to save you. The Department of Education and Ofsted certainly aren't going to come to the rescue. If anything, the pressure they exert is only going to increase in the coming years as stress on the education system intensifies. The earthquake is coming. It's time to take action for yourself and your school.

Everything outlined in this book can be achieved in your school, and you can achieve it sooner than you think. That being said it won't be easy. Things that are worth having aren't easily attained, and if you want to adopt cloud technology, take advantage of mobile devices or begin leveraging big data you must be willing to work for it. Your school will excel, you'll free up time and teaching will become the joyous profession that it should be for your teachers. The steps on that journey are simple. Stay committed, engage with experts, and let go of what isn't working.

It is an incredible time to work in education because the opportunities that technology offers are remarkable. These opportunities have never before existed in history. Everyday you don't take advantage of them is a day of lost learning opportunities. There's a reason why you didn't put this book down after the first chapter, and it's because you're passionate about improving your school. Google Apps for Education, one of the leading cloud-based education platforms was released on the 28th August 2006, and much of this 'new' technology isn't even new. The time for learning has passed. The time for action has begun.

One Final Thing

There was a chapter in this book that almost didn't make it, not because I feared that it wasn't good enough, but because I was worried I was giving away my secrets for free. I decided to include it in the end, because I realised that the ideas within it are what have enabled me to deliver successful project after project, no matter where the school or what the situation when I first walked in. It's an insight that I developed a long time ago, through a lot of trial and error, and even more mistakes. Before I discovered this I struggled too. I spent a huge amount of time and energy but didn't get the results I expected. Things would become stressful and at times I suffered from burnout. It's one of the very principles that I've built my company on, and I see people failing in their use of technology all the time because they don't know this key concept.

I've even shared it with a few people close to me but it made little difference. I learnt that ideas are worthless without the right implementation. Today everyone has dozens of ideas. The power is in bringing them into reality.

Do you know the chapter I'm talking about? You might have spotted it straight away, or maybe you skimmed right over it. I'm not going to tell you which one it is. It is something that you have to discover on your own. When you find it you'll know. I do hope you find it.

You may choose to re-read this book. It's much easier to spot the second time around and if you find it you'll realise how much it can transform your school.

I leave you with a final challenge once you find it. Put it into practice. Knowing it and putting it into practice are two very different things, and you'll only see the immense transformational value it has when you do the latter. I can assure you it's no mumbo-jumbo BS. Putting it into practice has changed my own life, my career and my entire outlook on the world.

I hope you find it.

Bibliography

Bambrick-Santayo, P. and Peiser, B. (2012) *Leverage Leadership.* San Francisco: Jossey-Bass

Coates, S. (2015) *Headstrong: 11 Lessons of School Leadership.* Melton: John Catt

Coe, R. et al. (2014) *What Makes Great Teaching?* The Sutton Trust

Collins, J. (2001) *From Good to Great.* New York: HarperBusiness

Department of Education (2013) *Improving Efficiency in Schools.* Department for Education Publication

Gawande, A. (2010) *The Checklist Manifesto.* New York: Metropolitan Books

Gill, S. (2015) *Journey to Outstanding.* Kent: Writing Matters

Goleman, D. (1995) *Emotional Intelligence.* New York: Bantam Books

Gladwell, M. (2000) *The Tipping Point.* Boston: Little, Brown

Gladwell, M. (2009) *Outliers.* London: Penguin

Gladwell, M. (2009) *What the Dog Saw.* Boston: Little, Brown

Higgins, S. et al. (2014) *Developing Great Teaching*. Teacher Development Trust Publication

Hill, A. et al (2016) *How to Turn Around a Failing School*. Centre for High Performance Publications

Kerr, J. (2013) *Legacy*. London: Constable

Kirkup, C. (2005) Schools' use of data in teaching and learning. Annesley: DfES Publications

Oakleigh Consulting, (2010) *Financial Impact Assessment of the National College's School Business Manager Demonstration Projects*, Nottingham: National College for Leadership of Schools and Children's Services

OECD (2015) *Students, Computers and Learning*. OECD Publishing

PricewaterhouseCoopers, (2010) *Strategic Study of School Business Managers and School Business Directors*, Nottingham: National College for Leadership of Schools and Children's Services

PricewaterhouseCoopers, (2010) *Cost Benefit Analysis of the School Business Management Programme,* Nottingham: National College for Leadership of Schools and Children's Services

Robinson, K. (2001) *Out of Our Minds*. North Mankato: Capstone

Sahlberg, P. and Hargreaves, A. (2011) *Finnish Lessons*. New York: Teachers College Press

Sellen, P. (2016) *Teacher Workload and Professional Development in England's Secondary Schools*. Education Policy Institute Publication

Sinek, S. (2014) *Leaders Eat Last*. London: Penguin, Portfolio

Syed, M. (2010) *Bounce*. London: Fourth Estate

Syed, M. (2015) *Black Box Thinking*. London: John Murray

Acknowledgements

In my continued quest to improve education I would like to thank a whole cast of amazing people.

Charlotte Green for her ever-present and unflinching support over the years on the rollercoaster journey from starting LearnMaker to this very day. It's a cliche to say I couldn't have done it without you but then I really couldn't have done it without you. This book is another chapter in the life long adventure that we're on together.

Daniel Priestley. First his wealth of knowledge and expertise has enabled me to write this book by putting onto paper the concepts and ideas that have long been stuck in my head. More importantly I'd like to thank him for his conviction and belief that entrepreneurs can change the world, and his belief in my own ability to do that.

The whole team at Dent and the mentors on the

KPI programme for their priceless advice, expertise and support over the last year. It's an exciting and energising community that I feel privileged to now be a part of.

Lucy McCarraher and the team at Rethink Press for all the support in helping me produce this book. It's turned out very different from the first draft I sent to you back in July 2016 but your great advice and expertise was integral in the evolution of what that early manuscript went on to become.

James Hannam for founding LearnMaker with me and being such an integral part of the projects mentioned in this book. I wish you the best of luck in your new adventures.

I'd also like to give immense thanks to Lizzie Edwards, Andre Marcos, Fadela Hilali, Louise Mallam and Antoinette Oglethorpe for all your support, belief and ongoing inspiration. I really do have an A-team of people in you all.

Finally a shout out to Sonia Gill, Sarah Carroll, Pat Lynnes, Sari van Poelje and Anthony Gluyas for their timeless advice and support while I've been writing this book and building LearnMaker.

About the Author

JAY ASHCROFT is a best-selling author, international speaker and award winning entrepreneur.

Having been around technology since before he could walk or talk, it seemed impossible that Jay would settle into any other career than one that involved it. Education ran a close second, and after graduating University Jay spent a number of years teaching, first in music schools and then in inner-city state secondary schools.

In 2011, Jay took the opportunity join *Apple* and it was here where he combined his passions for education and technology. Jay worked with *Apple's* retail partners, turning a new store in one of England's most deprived areas into one of Europe's highest performers in only 12 months. Jay's expertise and practices were later incorporated into the company's training provision. Later, he stepped across into an education role and oversaw more than £2 million of Apple hardware deployed into schools, working with thousands of teachers in the process and learning about their struggles firsthand. In 2014, discontent with how little support schools had when getting to grips with new technology, Jay quit his career and invested his savings to found *LearnMaker*.

Today, Jay combines his expertise in technology, education and organisational development to personally support the improvement of numerous schools. Jay is a best selling author, an award winning entrepreneur, and is asked to speak across the globe on the role technology plays in the future of education.

Jay is also the author of the book The Tablet Revolution: How to Transform Student Learning with iPad

The Accelerated School Improvement Programme

The Accelerated School Improvement Programme is a twelve-week development programme designed for forward thinking schools who want to accelerate their performance through simple and effective technology.

Over the course of the programme, we implement, transition and support your school as you adopt Google Suite for Education, the world's #1 education cloud-based platform. Not only will you have a whole new set of cutting edge tools at your disposal, more importantly, you'll be able to work in new ways that will raise the capability of your teachers, improve the productivity of your school and develop greater consistency across every lesson.

It is designed to help you implement the three key principles covered in this book. We support you along every step of your transition by delivering onsite training sessions, leadership coaching, implementation days, online webinars as well as providing access to a custom built eLearning platform. You'll work with experts in their fields and join a invite only community of forward thinking educators who've been through the programme.

This book stresses the importance of expertise and high quality implementation. The programme is designed as a journey that will enable your school to reach new levels of performance. Hundreds of teachers are already benefiting from the dramatic acceleration in school improvements after adopting Google Suite for Education. We provide high quality resources to speed up your progress, and after working with thousands of educators, we've discovered numerous strategies that create faster results for you. This is just one of the reasons why we are accredited and work directly with Google and The Department of Education.

Schools who participate in the Accelerated School Improvement programme consistently tell us that the experience was a catalyst for drastic improvements, far exceeding what they thought possible.

For more information on The Accelerated School Improvement Programme visit: www.learnmaker.co.uk

Get in Touch

If you would like to contact us in person you can get in touch with us on any of the ways below:

Website: www.learnmaker.co.uk
Email: hello@learnmaker.co.uk
Phone: 0121 270 7531

Additional Resources

We covered a lot of ground in this book, and as you take your first steps into accelerating your own school's improvement through simple and effective technology, we have produced several resources to support you further:

Free Online Resources

Find out more about the concepts covered in this book with our free resources at: www.learnmaker.co.uk/resources

The LearnMaker Scorecard

The first step to accelerating your school's performance begins in assessing where you're currently at. This is why we developed the LearnMaker Scorecard, a free online diagnostic tool that will score you on the three principles covered in this book. On completion you'll receive a customised, in-depth report with feedback on ways to improve further. Visit: www.learnmaker.co.uk/scorecard

Book a Discovery Session

If you'd like to speak about how you can accelerate your school's performance in person, book a complimentary Discovery Session. This is a sixty minute session with a senior member of the LearnMaker team where you will:

Gain Clarity by discovering where you're at and where you want go.

Gain Focus by pinpointing what is complex and ineffective about your current technology.

Gain a Plan to accelerate your performance through simple and effective technology.

Visit: www.learnmaker.co.uk/discovery-session

A Final Ask

I hoped you've enjoyed this book, and that the ideas, anecdotes and stories I've shared in it have given you a new insight into how we can transform education if we rethink the role technology plays.

To transform education we need a movement, and to create a movement we need to spread the word. If you enjoyed this book I'd like to ask for a few minutes in return. Open your phone, tablet or laptop and write a review on Amazon, or write a blog post or just spread the word via social media.

Every movement was started by just a handful of individuals. Small actions lead to big results, and your words can help spread the ideas I've put forward in this book. If we rethink how we use technology in our schools then we can transform education. All we need to do is reboot and a bright future will lay ahead.

Made in the USA
Charleston, SC
09 March 2017